GYMNASTICS
RULES IN
PICTURES

Michael Brown

A Perigee Book

Perigee Books
are published by
The Putnam Publishing Group
200 Madison Avenue
New York, NY 10016

Library of Congress Cataloging-in-Publication Data

Brown, Michael, date.
Gymnastics rules in pictures/Michael Brown.
p. cm.
ISBN 0-399-51636-0
1. Gymnastics—Rules—Pictorial works. I. Title.
GV463.3.B76   1990   90-38961 CIP
796.44—dc20

Printed in the United States of America
1   2   3   4   5   6   7   8   9   10

ACKNOWLEDGMENTS

Special thanks to Julie Sickels, Amateur Athletic Union National Women's Gymnastics Chairman, who served as book consultant; Mike Jacki, Executive Director of the United States Gymnastics Federation; and Mike Earle, Director of Publications at the National Collegiate Athletic Association, for their efforts and contributions to this book.

CONTENTS

FOREWORD

To the casual spectator, gymnastics might seem elegantly simple, but this surface beauty and simplicity can be deceptive. As an observer, you really need to know many technical details to appreciate the beauty and power of gymnasts going through their paces. Months of practice and years of training go into each performance. Athletes need to be aware of the official rules of gymnastics in order to progress in the sport. And while spectators may not *need* to know all the details, a greater knowledge of how gymnastics is evaluated can only lead to a deeper enjoyment of the sport. Almost all the details of gymnastics events and the equipment are covered in the official rules which are excerpted at the back of this book.

This guide is designed to help anyone new to gymnastics—athletes, coaches, spectators, parents—who'd like to have an overview of the rules. The pictorial format and simple language should make the basic rules and ingredients of gymnastics events clear even to novices.

At gymnastics events below the national level, many of the people who organize and administrate events—chairmen, technical directors, and so forth—are volunteers. These people are a vital component of the U.S. gymnastics program. (Coaches and judges, however, are usually paid for their efforts and contributions.) This volume might serve as a good first guide for anyone considering taking a volunteer role in their local gymnastics scene.

For gymnasts themselves, a knowledge of the rules and requirements cannot increase strength and stamina or enhance gracefulness, but gymnastics is highly regulated and a budding gymnast must be familiar with these regulations just as they must condition their bodies.

If the time spent with this book increases your enjoyment—whether as a spectator or a participant—of a sport that is continually growing in popularity in the U.S., or gives you some knowledge that helps you prepare for or succeed in a competition, it will have been time well spent.

While this book does not attempt to explain or illustrate every rule for every event, it does provide an overview of the most important aspects of the sport. If you'd like to know more about one of the points we cover, the complete official rules are available through the USGF at: Pan Am Plaza, Suite 300, 201 S. Capitol Avenue, Indianapolis, IN 46225. However, anyone who has tried to plow through the official rule book of any sport knows those regulations can leave nonlawyers shaking their heads. We hope that our text and pictures will make clear some of the more complex points, and that this volume as a whole will provide a painless introduction for the novice and an entertaining refresher for those with more experience.

INTRODUCTION

The Early History

As competitive sport, simple exercise, or just recreation, gymnastics is one of the most natural of activities. Take a healthy, energetic group of youngsters and let them loose on an open lawn of mowed grass and it will not be long before they invent some game that includes tumbling, jumping, cartwheels, and somersaults—do-it-yourself gymnastics. So it is not surprising that, while modern forms of gymnastics have only been practiced for the last hundred years or so, the basics of the sport have roots in antiquity.

Some of the world's oldest cultures, such as Egypt and China, left illustrated records of some of the movements that are part of the basics of gymnastics. Similar records exist even earlier in cave paintings showing figures performing acrobatic feats. It is likely that these activities existed purely as entertainment, not as the competitive events of today.

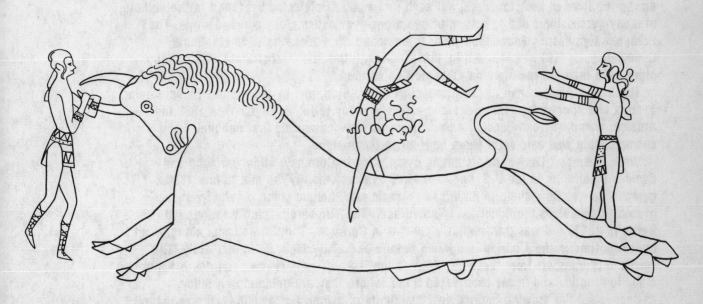

Artist's depiction of a restored fresco from the palace of Cnossus in Crete, showing acrobats performing somersaults over a bull.

For greater similarities to our modern form, we must look later to the Greeks, the culture that even introduced the word *gymnasia* to describe a building used for physical training. In Greece, gymnastics existed 2000 years before the first Olympics of 776 B.C. All-male events illustrated in frescoes dating from at least that long ago on the Island of Crete show acrobats vaulting over swords and the horns of bulls. However, like the Egyptian and prehistorical versions, these early games probably were not actually games or sports, but forms of physical training to prepare athletes for other competitive endeavors. These gymnastics had no system of scoring and none of the standardized equipment that gymnastics uses today.

When the military-minded Romans succeeded the Greeks in power, they continued to conduct Olympic Games. Not surprisingly, the Romans used gymnastics primarily as a form of training for soldiers. However, one facet of their training included wooden horses, used for practicing rapid mounting and dismounting. It is likely that the "horse" bodies used today in the vault and pommel events are the descendants of this piece of Roman equipment.

In A.D. 393 the Romans declared the Games corrupt and too Greek in origin and abolished them. With the fall of the Roman Empire and the beginning of the Dark Ages (500–1000), athletics and many other recreational activities were largely abandoned. Part of the reason was that the Christians favored spiritual activities over physical activities. Physical conditioning belonged solely in the domain of soldiers and knights. Knights in full armor, in fact, continued to practice on wooden horses. The gymnastics that existed was left to bands of acrobats and minstrels that entertained at fairs. These entertainers were probably solely responsible for developing and keeping the exercises alive through the end of the Middle Ages (1500). It was also during this era that women joined in as gymnastic dancers performing to music.

Physical activity regained some of its respectability in the Renaissance (1350–1650), but it was not until the late eighteenth century that gymnastics was reborn, this time in Germany. A handbook of gymnastics for the young, building on and adding to the old Greek exercises, was published there by Guts Muth and translated into many languages. In the following decades two men, the German, Johan Jahn, and the Swede, Pehr Ling, took Muth's general principles and encouraged a real reemergence of physical training and gymnastics.

Jahn was spurred by patriotism to improve the moral and physical condition of his fellow Germans, with something of an emphasis on brute strength. Ling's approach, on the other hand, left room for grace and the free flow of movement. The two approaches were at odds during the lives of their founders, but each had many disciples and resulted in the building of many gymnasiums and formation of numerous gymnastics clubs across Europe. The European Gymnastics Foundation (later to be called the Federation of International Gymnastics, or FIG) was founded in 1881, making it the first international sports group, older even than the International Olympic Committee.

The British Army began to use gymnastics for training, and by the middle 1800s training centers had opened for gymnastics instructors in many towns in England. In 1888 the Amateur Gymnastic and Fencing Association was founded and its first national championship was held eight years later in Northhampton.

While Jahn and Ling were promoting gymnastics in Germany, other Germans and Swedes emigrating to the U.S. began to open gymnasiums. By the mid to late 1800s, gymnastics was flourishing in America at a rapid rate, helped along greatly by such gymnastics clubs as the Sokols and Turnvereins. The Turnvereins club was founded in Berlin in 1811, and was tremendously popular in Germany. The Sokols came along about the same time in the Austrian-Hungarian empire and also caught on immediately. The waves of immigrants from those countries to the U.S. in the next two centuries brought the clubs to America and firmly established them, where they are going strong today.

Because of the growing international popularity of gymnastics activities, it was natural that they should be included on the program of the first revived international Olympic Games.

Gymnastics in the Modern Olympic Era

Only five countries sent gymnasts to the Olympics of 1896. The events were the horizontal bar, rings, and vault, and the contestants were exclusively male. Not surprisingly, considering their passion for gymnastics in the preceding century, the German team took most of the honors at those first Games.

Gymnastics continued to be part of the Games and for the next several decades, more and more countries began to send participants. The conditions under which the events were conducted, however, were haphazard at best: a given event might or might not be held, and when it was, its makeup varied; certain events might be compulsory at one competition, not at the next; and most surprising to modern sensibilities, teams often brought their own apparatus, which didn't always conform to the norm. In 1928 women competed for the first time, though only in a single event. The inclusion of this single event, a team rhythmic dance event, caused some controversy, and in 1932 once again women were not allowed to compete. Also in 1932 the number of competing countries decreased back down to five, due in part to a dire economic and political situation throughout the world. In 1936 women were back with every event but the floor exercise; women's competitions in the Olympics were not accepted or taken seriously, however, until 1952 when a strong showing by the Soviet women showed that the women were there to stay.

The year 1952 marked the beginning of some sweeping changes in gymnastics. First, the Soviets competed at Helsinki for the first time, and they took nearly every winning place in men's and women's events—twelve out of sixteen places—injecting some new excitement into the proceedings. Also, this year saw women's individual floor events in the Games for the first time. And something else was noticed in both men's and women's events: a movement away from an emphasis on power and strength toward beauty and grace. An element of dance, even choreography, had entered gymnastics.

Finally, at the very next Games in Australia in 1956, the program of events was stabilized, and that order is still used today: vault, uneven bars, balance beam, and floor exercise for women and floor exercise, pommel horse, still rings, vault, parallel bars, and horizontal bar for men. More rhythmic modern techniques of gymnastics, with their greater emphasis on rhythm, continued to be refined through the next several decades, and the Soviet Union, Eastern Europe, and Japan have continued to dominate many events.

TODAY'S COMPETITIONS

Gymnastics exist outside the Olympic Games, of course. There is a lively program of clubs, meets, and competitions at the local, regional, and national levels in the U.S. This program serves not only as a wonderful opportunity for physical education for youngsters, but as the training ground for future Olympians. A conservative estimate today is that 2 million people in the U.S. participate in gymnastics.

However, as in the case with other sports that are not highly professionalized— swimming, for instance, and many track and field events—the Olympic Games serve as the ultimate measuring stick. Before the Olympic level is reached, there is a complete competitive structure and organization governing gymnastics.

Internationally, the Federation of International Gymnastics (FIG) headquartered in Switzerland governs the sport. FIG helps organize most competitions between two or more nations, including the Olympics. FIG is generally regarded as the ultimate authority in gymnastics.

The national body recognized by FIG in the U.S. is the United States Gymnastics Federation (USGF). In addition to organizing exhibitions and national competitions, the USGF publishes a bimonthly magazine and is a source of information about the sport. The address is given in the foreword to this book.

The USGF in turn oversees some of the gymnastics activities of such groups as the Amateur Athletic Union (AAU) and the United States Association of Independent Gymnastics Clubs (USAIGC), as well as classes and tournaments sponsored by YMCAs, YWCAs, and other groups throughout the U.S. The National Collegiate Athletic Association (NCAA) and the National Federation of State High Schools Association (NFHSA) also conduct their own gymnastics programs in loose conjunction with the USGF.

Each of these groups has its particular function, serves different age groups, and maintains minor variations in the rules, all of which are coordinated with the USGF. It is perhaps confusing that many of these organizations also hold their own competitions for a national championship. As a result, there are many "national" U.S. champions, making one wonder who is the real champ. The answer is really quite simple: While the various organizations may use their national championships as qualifying meets to determine champions, the *official* national champions are given their titles at the "USGF Championships of the U.S.A."

A Unique Sport

Gymnastics is an unusual sport and there are many intricacies of performance and scoring involved in understanding the sport as it is practiced today.

It is true that gymnastics competitions at the Olympic level established a program in the late 1950s that generally has been followed since. However, this does not mean that for the last 30 years national and international gymnastics programs have been written in stone. The Olympic Committee is constantly fine-tuning the makeup of the gymnastics competition, and every 4 years FIG devises an altered set of compulsory exercises and of specifications for the equipment. (Compulsories are sets of exercises, to be done on the floor or on apparatus, that are determined by committee and which all contestants must perform in the same order and manner.) All contestants in international events must adhere to these specifications. The USGF also sets and alters compulsories at various skill levels for the competitions below the national level. Gymnasts of all ages in most of the different organizations strive to meet these skill levels and perform the recommended sets of compulsories.

Gymnastics is continually changing—much more so than nearly any other sport. Today women compete in four events (vault, uneven parallel bars, balance beam, and floor exercise) and men in six (floor exercise, pommel horse, still rings, vault, parallel bars, and horizontal bar). However, the level of accomplishment and the type and complexity of the ingredients of each routine is constantly changing. While a young woman's performance on the uneven parallel bars might last roughly the same amount of time as it did 20 years ago, the nature of her movements—the makeup of the routine—has changed dramatically.

In both women's and men's gymnastics, the development of an original skill (a new type of movement) is highly prized. In both men's and women's events, an important original skill is usually named after the athlete who developed it. Additionally, in international competition the persons who perform a new skill are awarded .2 points for originality.

As time and competitions go by and more and more athletes perfect a certain skill, its relative worth in the scoring decreases. The skill can eventually be "replaced" altogether by a related but newer, more original skill. In this way the sport achieves an incredibly vibrant identity. Gymnasts watch each other eagerly during competitions for the appearance of new skills that may one day become standard.

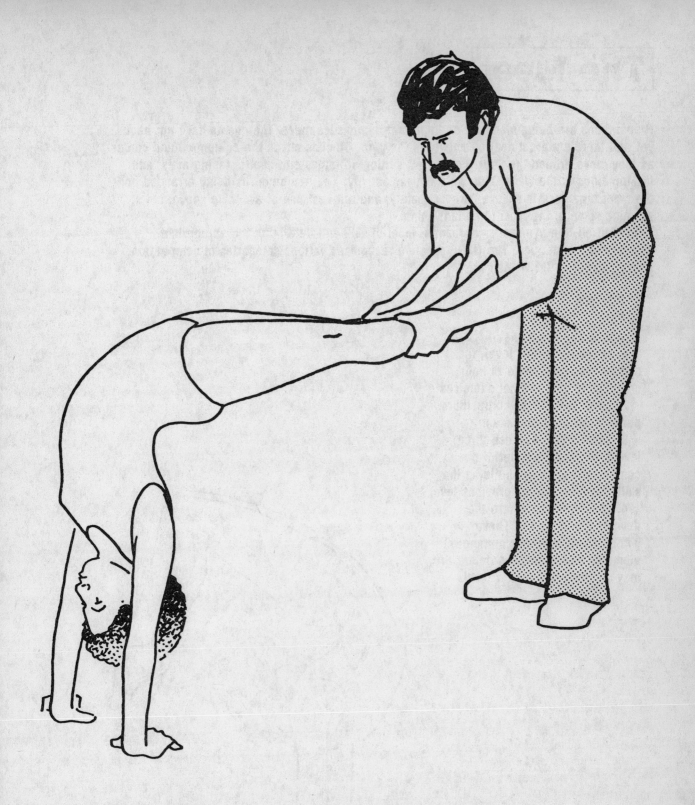

To underscore how much gymnastics differs from many other sports, imagine if every few years the NCAA decided, in basketball, to raise the basket, widen the court, or award four points for a backwards through-the-legs basket. It seems ludicrous. Gymnastics without change, however, would seem dead to those who love it.

Also, unlike many other team sports, one of the real joys of gymnastics is its emphasis on the individual's skill and improvement. Gymnasts work hard and train for months for those few moments at the meet when they have the chance to showcase their accomplishments.

The Meet

Preparations are being made for an important gymnastics meet. The events have not begun yet, but there's a great deal of activity in the gym. Officials check the equipment and confer as they move around the floor. People are setting up tables and chairs, taping mats, and tacking signs to the walls. This isn't aimless activity. The equipment is being arranged and the meet organized to ensure fairness, safety, and the best use of available space. Let's examine some of the most important points.

First of all, the gymnast's (or team's) level of skill will determine the appropriate category of competition. The USGF program recognizes various categories of competition. These categories for women are:

- Olympic
- Elite
- Age Group Programs

1. Level 10: At this level, the competitors must perform both compulsory and optional exercises.

2. Level 8–9: These competitors perform optional exercises.

3. Level 5,6,7: At these three levels, the gymnasts perform compulsories, always building the skills mastered in the previous level.

4. Level 1–4: These are the developmental levels. These gymnasts must master numerous elements and sequences before they may compete at a higher level.

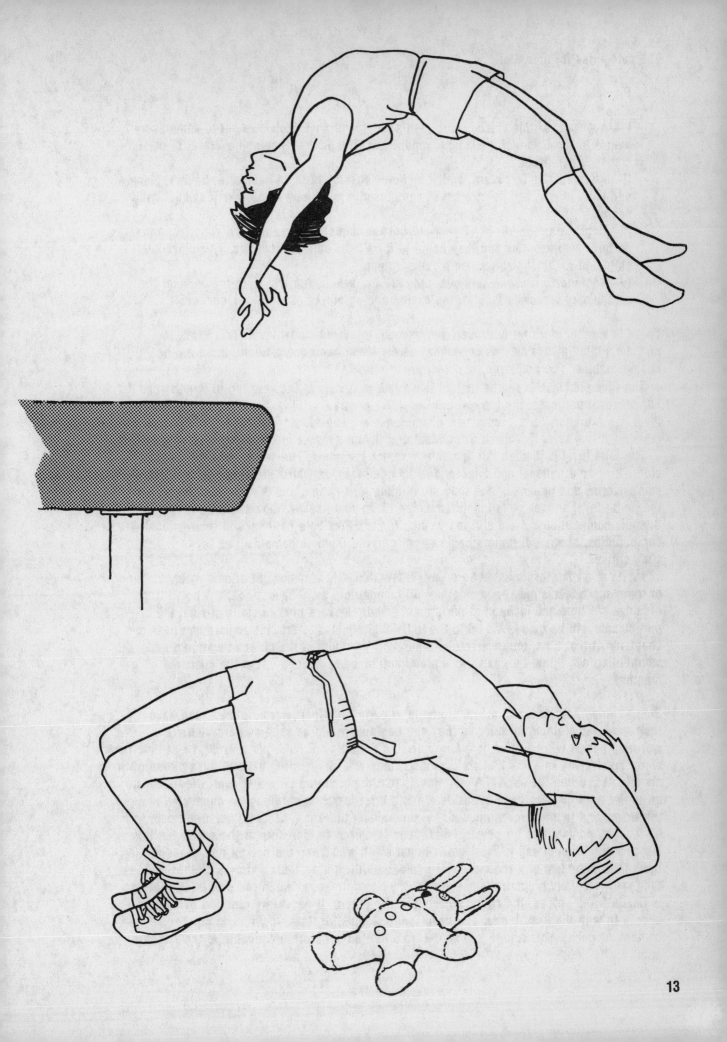

The categories for men are:

- Olympic
- Elite
- I—Advanced: At this class, young men aged 15–19 have their own set of compulsory events in local through national competitions. This is the "beginning" level of most star U.S. gymnasts.
- II—Intermediate: This class, which includes boys of 12 to 14 years old, holds regional and local meets, has its own set of compulsories, and may employ various qualifying scores.
- III—Beginners: The 10- to 12-year-old boys in this class have enough experience to perform compulsories and they begin to form their optional routines. This class holds state and regional championship competitions.
- IV—Beginners: These 7- to 9-year-olds are the true beginners. Here they master the compulsory exercises that are the basic building blocks of all the higher levels.

There is another class for both men and women, the recreational level. This level, for noncompetitive gymnastics, is conducted purely for fun and exercise and there are no championships. The programs vary from area to area.

The Olympic class is shared by just those few gymnasts at the very top of their skills. For practical purposes, the top level in the USGF program is Elite. Excelling at the Elite level is a prerequisite to becoming a championship gymnast, since it is from the pool of athletes at this level that the U.S. national and Olympic teams are chosen.

The Elite level is divided into junior and senior programs. The seniors are 15 years or older; they hold national and international competitions, in which they perform the Olympic compulsories and optionals, and they are eligible for Olympic and World competitions. In the junior level are top young athletes under 15. In some cases, they might be ready for Olympic competition but are still too young. Junior Elites hold national and international competitions; at age 14, juniors begin to perform the Olympic compulsories in competitions.

Meets at all the levels listed here have a few things in common. At a team meet, 2, 3, 4 or many more teams may be competing. All competitors must have a coach, who will organize the time and location of performance and take care of the details of what the participants will be doing. It's up to the individual athletes to find the registration desk and check in. At that time, they are issued a number; printouts of the order of warm-up and competition will either be posted in a prominent place or handed out at the coaches' meeting.

Smart competitors arrive at meets promptly or early, find their warm-up area, and have their gear and clothing in order so they can begin warm-up as soon as permitted. The warm-up period will be brief, just a minute to a minute and a half per entrant. Or, if time to warm up is given in a block to six gymnasts, they will all warm up at once for a period of six minutes. When the meet director signals that the warm-up period is over, the gymnasts go to the area that has been set aside. Then a brief march-in ceremony is conducted and the teams and judges are introduced. In some meets there is a separate warm-up area, to be used by competitors for physical warm-ups just prior to their turn at the event, but this is not a requirement and in most cases is not available. When the person just ahead of them is in the midst of a routine, most gymnasts will remove their warm-up clothes and, as they wait, mentally prepare themselves for their performance. When the preceding routine is finished and judged, the coach adjusts the equipment, if necessary, and the gymnast checks in with the head judge. The head judge signals for the competitor to go. The competitor must acknowledge this signal from the judge before proceeding to the starting point.

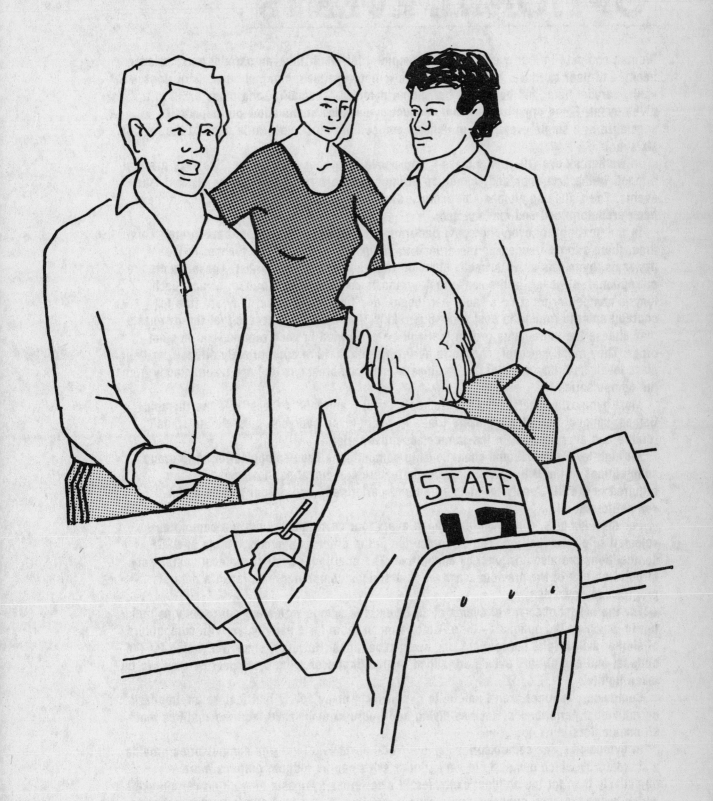

COMPULSORY AND OPTIONAL EVENTS

Women compete in four events, in the Olympic order: vault, uneven parallel bars, balance beam, and floor exercise. Men compete in six: floor exercise, pommel horse, still rings, vault, parallel bars, and horizontal bar. Some gymnasts specialize, and many excel in a given event. Some organizations that conduct gymnastics meets allow participants to specialize in a single event, but in general competitors must perform in each of the four or six events.

In women's Level 10, men's Class I, and above, two phases of competition take place at a meet. In the first, men and women go through compulsory versions of the six and four events. The skills and elements of exercise that must be shown in each compulsory have been predetermined and may not vary.

In the next phase, everyone again performs each event, but in an optional format. This time, there's more freedom in the order and composition of the performance. In the optionals, gymnasts strive to really show off their abilities to the utmost. These events are not optional, however, in the sense that gymnasts can choose to do them or not. Each female competitor must do a vault, bar, beam, and floor routine, but they are free to choreograph the routine to best show their skills. The optional aspect is that the gymnasts may choose the ingredients (skills) that will be performed in each routine, and in what order. They must, however, choose to perform skills that are appropriately difficult for their class level, and they may not use routines or skill combinations that are taken exactly from the compulsories.

Most gymnastic meets, from the women's Level 5 and men's Class IV to the Olympic Games, conduct sets of compulsory trials. At every level, everyone must do the same routine and every entrant in the same class must perform.

All high-level international championship competitions have compulsories. Age group competitions in the U.S. almost universally feature compulsories; however, they are required in the NCAA only for male all-around performers, and not for female NCAA competitors at all.

For the Olympics, compulsories change every four years, according to a committee selected solely for that job. The compulsories in the different age/class levels in USGF competitions are also designed by committee. The goal is for each class level compulsory to build on that of the previous class, so that serious competitors can make a natural progression upwards.

For the casual observer of events at all levels, the compulsories are not usually as much fun to watch as the optionals—there isn't as much room for creativity, so with competitors of similar skill levels, the routines can seem repetitious. However, since the scores for the optional and compulsory events are added for the final score, the compulsories aren't to be taken lightly.

Compulsory routines aren't unique to gymnastics; many sports that feature an emphasis on individual performance, such as diving and figure skating, have required routines that all competitors must do.

In gymnastics, the compulsories serve several purposes. First, the compulsories provide a standard by which gymnasts of very similar skills can be judged, perhaps more objectively than for the optional exercises. It also forces gymnasts to work on certain skills, which keeps the sport cohesive and makes it possible for the best minds in gymnastics to help guide the evolution of the sport. Finally, some nations tend to favor the abolition of the compulsories, finding them restraining, while other competitors welcome the guidance and discipline provided by the universal sets of exercises. The USSR, for instance, historically has excelled in compulsories, and this helps them to hold a dominant position.

All-Around and Team Titles

A woman or girl gymnast who competes in a meet possibly could win one to four events. Men and boys might win anywhere from one to six. But there is one final award available to both sexes, and that is title of all-around, a measure of all-around excellence. Along with team titles, the all-around title, is highly prized. It does not represent a separate event but is decided by the combined scores from all the other events. A gymnast need not win every or even the most events; the total score is what matters.

A gymnast's individual score is determined by a scoring system called the Code of Points. This Code assigns a point value to every aspect of a gymnast's routine in each event. It also outlines what is or is not allowed during competition. The Code is very detailed and specific, so most people find it very complicated, but this system provides a fairer way of judging each gymnast than existed in the past. For more detailed information on scoring, see the scoring and judging section of this book on page 44.

Team titles are also highly prized, and like the all-around championships, they are determined by a totalling of scores. In general, the total is derived from combining the top scores on each event from among the team's members. (The exact procedure for determining team winners varies at different levels.) Even though a gymnastics team is not "out there on the court" all at once like a basketball team, they train together, provide each other support, and like any other team, pull together to come out on top and be number one.

AN EXPLANATION OF THE INDIVIDUAL EVENTS

The Language of Gymnastics

As with any sport, there's a special language required when discussing the movements of that sport. In gymnastics we describe various skills as "elements." There are elements of strength (the iron cross, for example), of balance (a handstand is one), or of flexibility (such as a split). Elements are also referred to as swinging, flight (in which the gymnast lets go of the apparatus or floor and flies free for an instant), holding (which requires holding a certain position for a given number of seconds), or transitional (moving from one skill to the next).

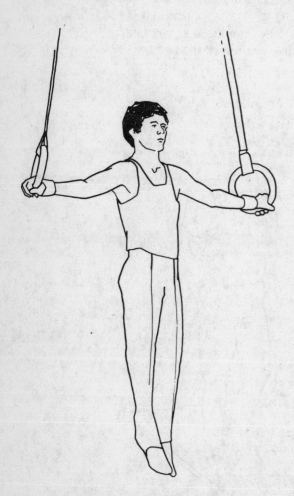

#1   *strength and holding elements*

#2   *balance element*

#3 flexibility element

#4 swinging element

#5 flight element

Sometimes an element may combine several qualities—strength *and* balance, for example. If an optional routine requires one element of skill and one of strength, a single element will satisfy both in some cases, and in other cases will not. There are a variety of elements at many skill levels from which gymnasts may choose to design their optionals. They must, however, meet the general requirements of elements for their class. In the compulsories, of course, the components and order required for each class are specifically listed.

Other bits of gymnastics jargon are *direction changes* (there are three: forward, backward, and sideways) and the *body wave* (which can be either frontward, backward, or sideways. In a body wave, the gymnast bends in one of these directions, contracts the body tightly, then in a smooth motion releases the hips, upper body, and head—in this order—slowly out and up.) A *split* refers to a position in which one leg is extended forward and the other backward at right angles to the torso. *Amplitude* is another word you'll hear often; it refers to the amount of extension of the parts of the body—height, as well as arm and leg reach.

These terms are only examples. As gymnasts progress they learn a special language all their own to describe movements, skills, and elements. Like any other language, it will build up slowly until the athlete finds that she or he must provide translation for "outsiders."

#6   amplitude

Individual Events

What follows is a description of the men's six and women's four events. These are only general requirements that apply to both optional and compulsory events. The compulsories of each class level are made up of specific elements that must be performed in a specific order. We can't list every compulsory skill, but the general requirements for each event are described here. The optional routines also follow these general requirements but they are more flexibly structured. A gymnast will be penalized, however, if the optionals do not conform to the requirements of the compulsory skills or if the difficulty of the skills does not match the gymnast's performance level.

The required difficulty of the skills will vary greatly among the various classes of competition. For instance, for the men's rings exercise, at least one element of strength must be held for two seconds. This is true for the Elite as well as the Beginner athlete, but the difficulty of that element will differ.

MEN'S EVENTS

Men's Floor Exercise

Apparatus: Not just any old floor will do. To prevent injury and aid in the execution of the exercises, a gymnastics floor must be extraordinarily resilient and flexible. The floor is constructed of layers of plywood with either rubber/foam blocks or springs; this construction is then covered with 1¼-inch ethofoam and carpet. The competition area is 40 feet × 40 feet with a 2-foot border for safety.

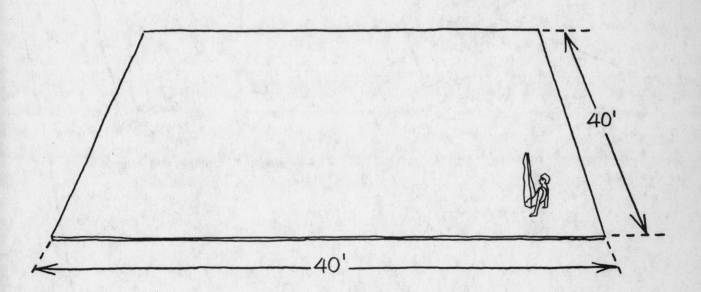

The Event: The gymnast performs the skills of the floor exercise in a free-form manner, leaping, tumbling, somersaulting without the aid of apparatus. The gymnast must make use of the whole floor during his exercise. The exercise must last at least 50 to 70 seconds, and he's required to do:

- three or four tumbling passes in at least two directions. A tumbling pass is a series of skills. It starts with a run, includes several skills one right after the other, and winds up with a final skill to punctuate the pass. Often these passes include acrobatic saltos, which are complete 360-degree head-over-heels rotations of the body in the air. The salto must reach at least head height. In a double salto, the body makes two rotations before touching down, and a twisting salto includes a side-to-side rotation of the body. Note: The best high-level gymnasts perform tumbling passes of great difficulty, almost always including twisting double saltos.

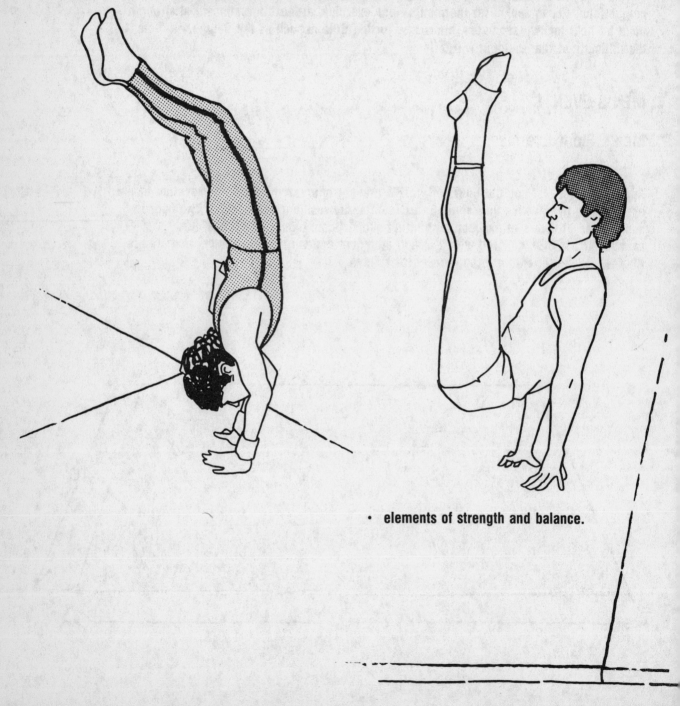

- **elements of strength and balance.**

- transitional skills of proper harmony and rhythm (transitional skills are those movements used to link other movements).

Men's Pommel Horse

Apparatus: The horse is 4 feet high, 14 inches wide, and 5 feet long. The pommels are real or synthetic wood and the body is made of wood and/or steel covered in a thick padding. It is upholstered with real or synthetic leather.

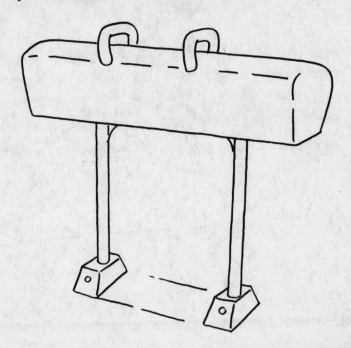

The Event: While supporting himself by one or both hands on the two "handles" (pommels), the gymnast must swing his body in unbroken, circular motions over the middle and both ends of the apparatus. There are two types of swings. Most of the routine is made up of circular swings in which the gymnast keeps his legs together and swings them in wide circles around his hands and the supports.

The other swing is the scissor swing, when the gymnast swings from side to side, usually with one leg on each side of the horse. During this event, these things are required:

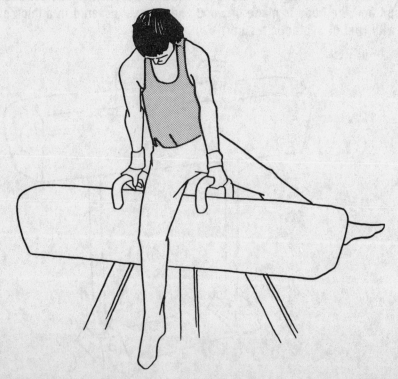

• scissors elements.

- **only hands touching the apparatus.**

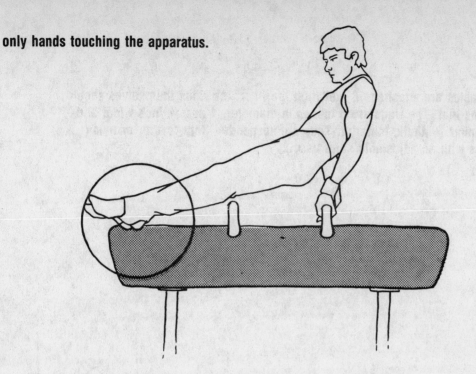

- **a steady, controlled rhythm.**

Note: The complicated hand and body positions of this exercise must seem to blend together effortlessly. This goal is made much more difficult by the fact that the gymnast is usually bearing his weight on just one arm, with the other arm always reaching toward the next skill. The hands should never appear to fumble and there should be no "seam" between one skill and the next. His body should never rest on the apparatus.

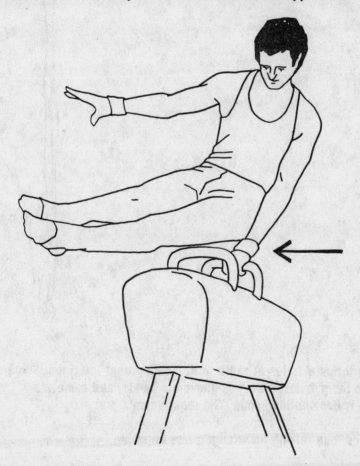

Men's Rings

Apparatus: The ring cables are attached 18 feet from the floor; the rings themselves should hang 8½ feet above the mat. The rings are 8 inches in diameter, 1 and ⅛ inch wide, and made of wood or a similar synthetic material. They are suspended from leather or nylon straps and steel cables with an adjustable steel base.

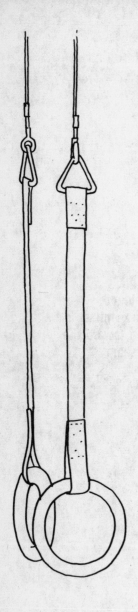

The Event: The gymnast performs a series of skills while holding onto the rings. Some skills are "support"—when the gymnast's body is above his hands, and some are "hanging," when his body is beneath his hands. The requirements are:

- two or more handstands, one relying on strength, one on swing.

- at least one element of strength held for at least 2 seconds. (Examples include a planche or front lever. A planche is a skill of strength and balance in which the gymnast supports himself on his hands above the rings, arms straight, body parallel to the floor or apparatus; a lever is similar, except the body is supported below the rings.)

- keeping the rings still during the movements—unnecessary swings and movement will cause deductions to be made.

Note: The most important quality of the performance is the stillness of the rings, which, given their instability, is no easy feat. Along with this stillness (the rings should not swing or quiver) it's important that the gymnast's body doesn't sag or twist and that his arms remain steady, unwavering throughout the performance. This takes a considerable amount of strength. The hallmark of a good performance is calm, steady movements. When holding his body parallel to the floor, he should stop still for the full 2 seconds and move gracefully onto the next skill. In swinging maneuvers, the body should be fully extended and the handstands straight.

Men's Vault

Apparatus: The body of the vault is 4½ feet high, 14 inches wide, and 5 feet long. The vault runway is 80 feet long and 3 feet wide. The body is made of wood and/or steel covered in a thick padding. Its nonslip surface is made of real or synthetic leather. There is also a special springboard for vaulting. It can be made of a variety of spring devices encased in a laminated wood sheet.

The Event: Male vaulters run along the runway and vault over the horse, which is placed parallel to the runway. (The women's vault is placed perpendicular to the runway.) Men's vaults are also called the long-horse vault. Gymnasts do a variety of vaults, depending on the level of competition. In general the gymnast runs up to vault and takes off the springboard (pre-flight), contacts the horse with the hands propelling the body into the actual vault of choice, and travels through the air (second flight), to the landing. In preliminary competitions, men perform one vault. The finalists with the highest scores then perform two vaults each and these two scores are averaged for a final score.

1.   2.   3.   4.   5.

The different parts of the men's vaulting horse were once separated into zones, but these are rarely referred to any longer. However, the gymnast must indicate beforehand which end of the horse he'll be using for his vault.

All vaults have names and are given a value in the Code of Points, the official text, used by judges, which gives the value of each skill. In addition, there are requirements about how high and far the gymnast must fly:

- in pre-flight, the gymnast must rise quickly, and by the time the hands reach the horse, the body must have obtained the proper angle.

- in the second flight, the body of the gymnast must reach at least a meter above the horse.

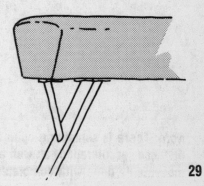

- he must land at least two meters from the end of the horse.
- the landing should be firm, should have no extra steps, and should fall in line with the horse, board, and runway, not over to the left or right.

Note: There is something open and large about a good vault. All the elements—height, distance, acceleration, as well as a firm, unwavering landing—create an impression of big movements done with complete ease.

Men's Parallel Bars

Apparatus: The bars, oval shaped in cross section, are made of real or synthetic wood covering steel-reinforced wood or fiberglass. The bars, which are 11 feet long, are adjustable and can be set from 16 to 20 inches apart. They are 6 feet from the floor.

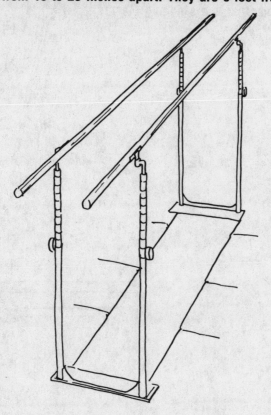

The Event: This routine includes swinging, flight, and hold elements—usually about 11 skills are shown. The gymnast performs somersaults, leg swings, and handstands as he holds and releases the bars with his hands. The execution of the mount and dismount are also important. Strength skills may be included, but are not mandatory. Specifically required are:

- swinging movements that work above and below the bar.

- at least one movement of superior difficulty that is a swinging element.

- the gymnast must release and regrasp the bars with both hands during a medium- or superior-difficulty move.

Note: Higher level gymnasts sometimes perform selected skills on a single bar. This isn't required, but will mark a good performance. Another mark of a good performance is front and back saltos, during which the gymnast loses sight of the bars for an instant. The more of these performed, the more difficult the routine.

Men's Horizontal Bar

Apparatus: This stainless-steel bar is 1⅛ inch in diameter, 8 feet long, and stands 8 feet above the floor on semi-adjustable steel uprights.

The Event: Swing skills without stops in between are performed on the horizontal bar. The routines here look much different from the parallel bars, which include holding skills. On the horizontal bar, the emphasis is on the swings, which can also be referred to in general as "giant swings." Some specific requirements are:

- at least one move where the gymnast releases and regrasps the bar.

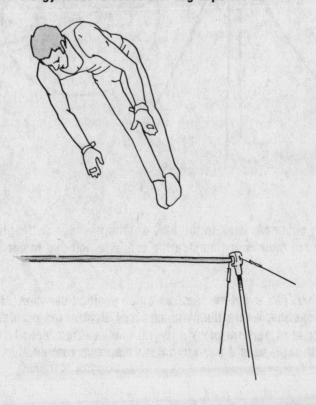

- at least one giant with either his back to the bar, or with an "el" or "eagle" grip (wrists rolled inward until thumbs are outside the grip and pointing in opposite directions).

Note: Also called the high bar, this event emphasizes quick position changes. Movements of special skill are the blind releases, where the gymnast loses sight of the bar during a salto or twist. Gymnasts have begun to perform many one-arm giant swings recently; many in succession is a mark of high skill, as is a one-arm/blind release in combination, and a "big" dismount.

WOMEN'S EVENTS

Women's Vault

Apparatus: The vault is 4 feet high, 5 feet long, and 14 inches wide. The vault runway is 82 feet long and 3 feet wide. The horse body is made of wood and/or steel covered in a thick padding. It is upholstered with real or synthetic leather with a non-slip surface. The springboard is laminated wood and any one of a number of spring devices. Women's vault is also sometimes called the side-horse vault.

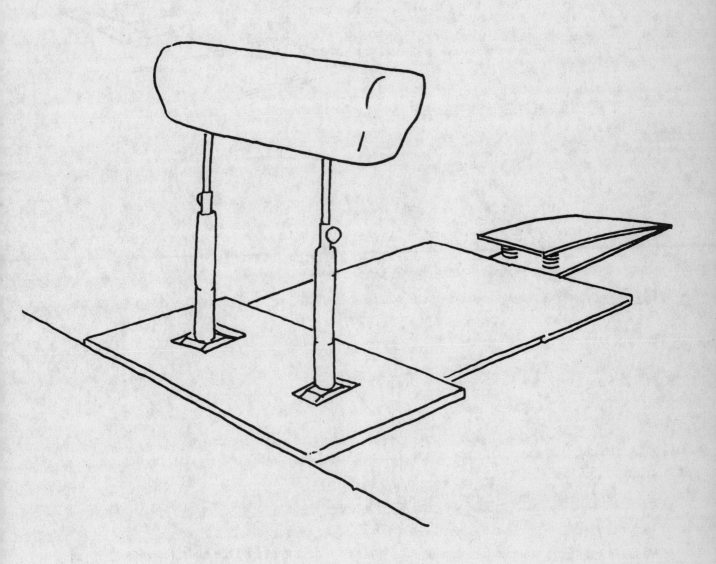

The Event: As in the men's vault, the women's vault consists of three basic parts: the gymnast runs up to vault and springs (pre-flight), contacts the vault with the hands propelling the body into the vault of choice, and travels through the air to the landing (second flight). For women's events, the vaults are placed perpendicular to the runway (men's are parallel).

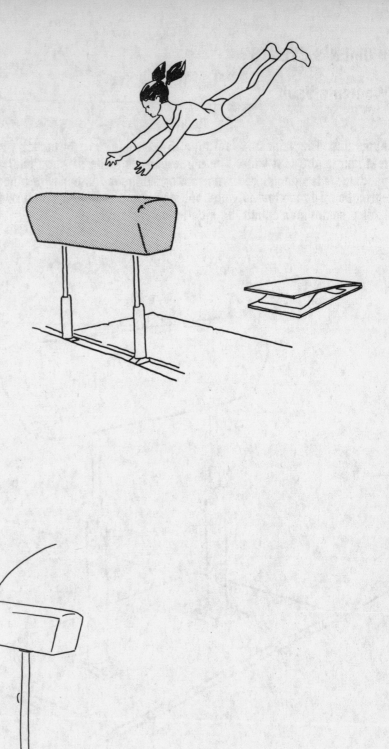

Women's vaults are grouped into 4 categories, which are determined by the body positions and movements of that vault. When a gymnast selects a vault, she must meet the requirements for that vault according to the Code of Points. In early rounds of competitions, gymnasts usually have two chances to do a vault, and the better score counts. In finals, though, she does two different vaults and the scores are averaged.

Note: Here are some ingredients of a successful vault: strong, explosive run; feet going quickly up over the head; proper body, shoulder, and hand position when she pushes off the horse; and an instantaneous push-off. A good second flight is also important—the better height and distance and the more twists and saltos, the higher-difficulty and more challenging the vault. A steady, snappy landing is also critical.

Women's Uneven Bars

Apparatus: These bars, oval shaped in cross section, are 8 feet long. The lower bar is 5 feet from the floor; the higher one is 8 feet. The bars may be raised, both by the same increment, for very tall women. The bars are wood surfaced and on the inside is steel-reinforced wood or fiberglass. The adjustable uprights and the base are steel. The bars may be moved apart slightly to accommodate the size of the gymnast.

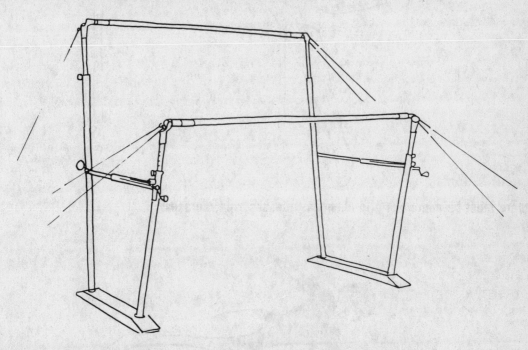

The Event: Like the men's horizontal bar, the emphasis on this event is movement elements—swing, flight, changes of elements—rather than holds. The general requirements are:

- gymnast must use both upper and lower bars;

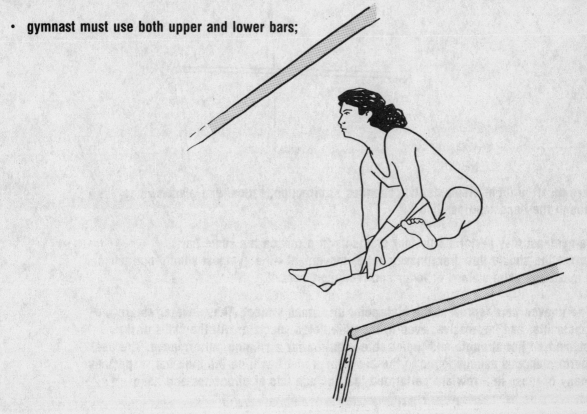

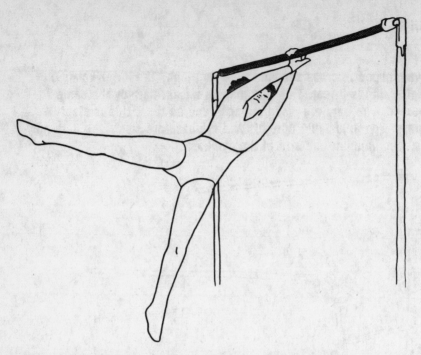

- there must be numerous grip changes, releases, and regrasps;

- there must be flight elements, two changes of direction, saltos, and giant swings through the handstand position;

- the gymnast may perform only four elements in a row on the same bar;
- the routine should flow from movement to movement—the gymnast should not pause or make any extra swings or falter and resupport herself.

Note: The uneven bars represent the high point of women's meet. These exercises are the most spectacular and impressive, even to the uninitiated spectator. All the skills of the gymnast, and all her strength and timing, are required for a shining performance. The peak of the performance is usually found in the big swings that begin on the high bar, especially when many of these in a row are performed that include lots of pirouettes and hand changes.

Women's Balance Beam

Apparatus: The 4-foot-tall balance beam is 16 feet long, but a mere 4 inches wide. It's made of wood, covered with a nonskid suede or suede-like material and rests on an adjustable steel base.

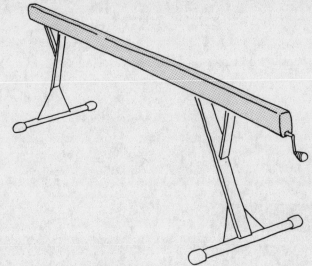

The Event: This event combines gymnastic, acrobatic, and dance movements. It is somewhat like the floor exercise, with the added interest of being performed up on such a narrow apparatus. In the 70 to 90 seconds allotted to her, the gymnast must use the entire length of the beam; she must also create high points, with two or more elements performed in a series. Specific requirements are:

• an acrobatic series that includes at least one flight element.

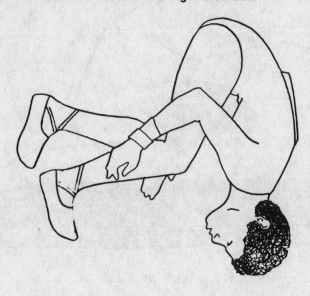

- a gymnastic leap or jump of great amplitude.

- a turn on one leg of at least 360 degrees.

- a series of gymnastic/acrobatic elements in at least two directions.
- a gymnastic series.
- one element close to the beam.

Note: The gymnast's effort to maintain balance should not be obvious as she performs—it should seem that she could just as well be on the floor. There should be a smooth transition, both from sitting to standing to leaping, and between the elements of the routine.

40

Women's Floor Exercise

Apparatus: The floor is constructed of layers of plywood with either rubber/foam blocks or springs attached. This construction is then covered with a 1¼-inch ethofoam elastic material and carpet. The area is 40 feet × 40 feet with a 1- to 2-foot border for safety.

The Event: Like the men's floor exercise, the women's is performed out in the open without any apparatus except the special floor. Unlike men's, women's floor exercises must always be choreographed to music during competitions. They also must last from 70 to 90 seconds, and she must cover the entire floor, using acrobatic and gymnastic elements to create peaks in the routine. Specifically there must be:

- three different acrobatic series with at least one salto.
- an acrobatic series with at least two or more saltos.

- an acrobatic/gymnastic series with great amplitude.
- a gymnastic series with considerable height and distance of movement.

It is most important that the gymnast blend all elements smoothly and make level and direction changes harmoniously.

Note: The most important quality of the gymnast's performance in this event is grace. She must use her great athletic ability to make the performance appear as effortless as dancing often appears; her movements should seem to be a single flow of motion matched to the movement, rather than a calculated accumulation of skills and exercises.

Women's Rhythmic Events

Another area of gymnastic endeavor for women that we have not mentioned up until now is women's rhythmic gymnastics. This has been recognized as a sport by FIG since 1962. As of yet, rhythmic gymnastics is not as popular in the U.S. as in other countries; however, it is catching on here.

The deductions spelled out by the Code of Points for the floor exercise also pertain to rhythmic events. The two are related, but the rhythmic events are better described as gymnastic dance and body movements performed with the following small equipment: rope, hoop, ball, clubs, and ribbons. Individual exercises last a minute to a minute and a half and take place on a carpet or wood floor measuring 40 feet by 40 feet.

Each routine must have four or more elements of superior difficulty and four or more of medium difficulty. These elements consist of using the equipment in various choreographed motions, such as swings, circles and figure-eight circles, tosses, catches, jumps, pivots, waves, rolls, and spins.

SCORING AND JUDGING

It only takes a few minutes for a novice basketball observer to understand the gist of that game's scoring system: whoever gets the most baskets wins. It takes a little more information to understand how all the compulsory and optional gymnastics routines are scored and the winners determined.

One important thing to know is that each of the skills in each of the sets of four and six events for women and men has a point value. This point value is an indication of how difficult that skill is to master or how original it is. These point values change as skills become universally accomplished at a certain level and their novelty lessens—one of the most important reasons for the constantly changing nature of gymnastics that we discussed earlier.

In optional events, skills are rated A, B, C, and D for difficulty, the D skills being the most difficult. Here's an example of how the ratings might apply to the different levels: in vaults, a top-level performer would almost never do a simple A vault, and only Elite and Olympic performers, because of the danger, are permitted to do D vaults. D vaults are usually round-off vaults, a recently developed vault that begins with a round-off onto the spring board.

Another unusual scoring method that fans of other sports might find startling is the fact that the scoring for compulsories doesn't start at zero and increase, it generally starts at 10 points and decreases as the performance progresses. A sport where the athlete can start out with a perfect 10!

In rare cases, gymnasts retain that perfect score by committing no errors and giving a flawless execution of a routine that requires the most advanced skills appropriate to their level. More commonly, the judges whittle down the score a bit for each flaw, mistake, or omission in the performance. As in most areas of life, perfection is rare.

Evaluating optional exercises is somewhat more difficult than compulsories. In compulsories, the judges know what the performer will do. Part of the evaluation is how well the gymnast follows the requirements, and the judge is thoroughly familiar with these requirements before the performance begins. This is not true for optionals, in which judges must wait and see what the gymnast is going to come up with, and then use the official judges' text—the Code of Points—to judge the performance.

There are some differences between how compulsory and optional exercises are judged. For one thing, all compulsory exercises are scored starting with 10 points, minus deductions. Exercises vary, however, in the number of starting points. Vaults have values from 9.0 to 10.0; the others begin at 9.6. The only way a gymnast can make 10 points in the optional exercises is to be awarded a .4 bonus for special content.

Optional and compulsory exercises do share common deductions for errors in similar situations. Also, some errors range in severity—a gymnast may show a moderate lack of amplitude, or a complete lack, and the amount of the deduction will range accordingly. Other errors will result in a single standard deduction each time they occur in any degree.

One difference in judging men's and women's gymnastics is that the individual judges' scores in men's competitions are open—that is, they are revealed for all to see. In women's competitions, however, the individual judges' scores remain closed, and all that is revealed is the final tabulated score. Another difference is that judges in men's contests tend to give higher scores for compulsories than for optionals, while judges of women's events judge the compulsories more rigorously, resulting in lower compulsory and higher optional scores.

In both the men's and women's methods, however, it is normal for four or more judges to come up with four different scores. How is that possible if the deductions are all defined and spelled out? For one thing, no matter how well trained the judges are, some kinds of deductions leave room for subjective appraisal. For instance, one judge may see a lack of amplitude where another judge does not. As you read further, other examples will be obvious.

For both men and women, the Code roughly divides the 10 points per performance in half—5 for substance (what the gymnast does) and 5 for form (how it is done).

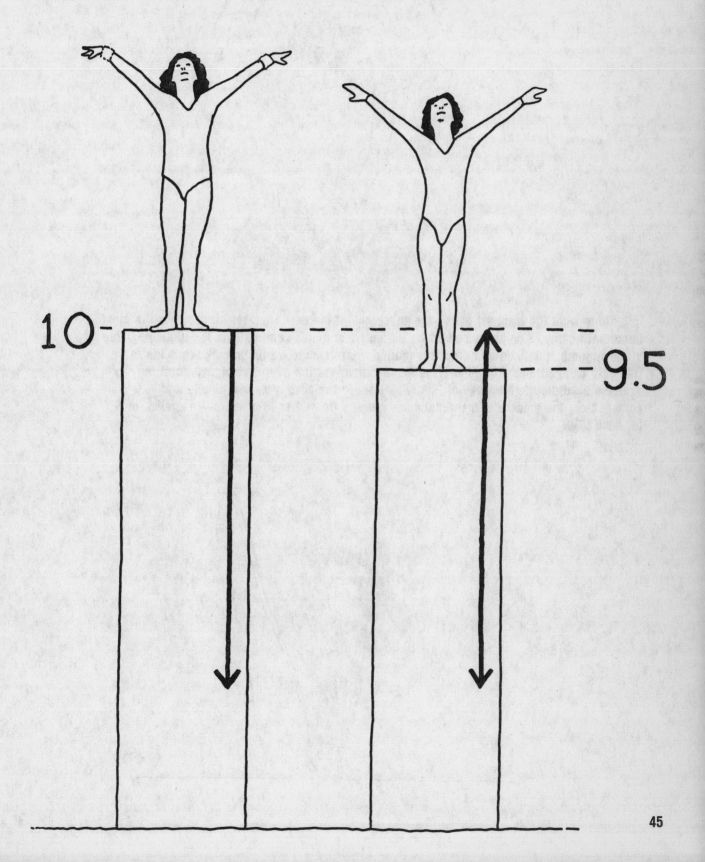

Substance

In judging what the gymnast does—the substance of the performance—difficulty is the most important quality: 3 points are given for difficulty. In men's competitions the difficulty value of movements is defined and precisely graded; more subjective judgments are made in women's competitions. The other 2 points are given for the overall composition of the exercise according to the Code of Points outline. In the case of both difficulty and composition, the amount of the deduction—ranging from .1 to .6 or more—is spelled out for each skill.

Form

The 5 points awarded for form are not as precisely defined. The judgment inevitably contains a subjective element, since the judges are actually rendering among other things an appraisal of the artistic merits of the performance.

Such qualities as elegance, appearance, bearing, and the ease and grace of the gymnast's movements are all considered.

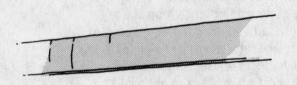

Even the appearance of the gymnast's garments will be considered.

When discussing form in gymnastics, the term "execution and amplitude" is constantly used to describe the form of the performance. Execution and amplitude might also be described as the shape and size of the movements. Execution errors might include bad head positioning, eyes down when they should be up, wobbles, and flat footedness. Amplitude, as we discussed earlier, is the amount of extension of the parts of the body— height, as well as arm and leg reach.

However you describe it, the important thing to remember is that it won't matter if a gymnast always includes every element and every degree of difficulty required—they may still get a low score, a very low one, in fact. The reason for this is that the height and grace of a leap is every bit as important, perhaps more so, than the mere fact that it was carried out. The performance doesn't merely need to be done, it needs to be done at the maximum height, with the straightest legs, and with the most open movements.

New gymnasts sometimes are baffled by an "unfair" low score. A young man on the pommel horse, for instance, knows he included all the right moves, never rested or leaned on the apparatus, and didn't fall when he dismounted, so why was his score so low? As he becomes more experienced, he'll know the answer. His movements were not graceful, his height and arm and leg reach were poor, his swings were small. It was a tight, small performance—lousy execution and amplitude.

For beginners, and in optionals at all levels, the biggest deductions are typically given for errors in execution and amplitude.

Common Mistakes of Beginners and Elite Athletes

In the *floor exercise,* new gymnasts tend to bend their knees or elbows when they should be straight; they often rush the rhythm and neglect to point their toes or keep their heads up. More experienced gymnasts might allow their ankles to wobble or take an extra, unnecessary step; they might express too much energy at an inappropriate moment or emphasize their most accomplished "stunts" at the expense of keeping high on their toes.

On the *parallel bars,* beginners might bend their arms and legs when they shouldn't, fail to give the routine a continuous feel, or take extra swings. More advanced performers, since they are attempting more difficult maneuvers, fall more often. They might also inadvertently allow their legs to separate when they should not; they also sometimes fail to perform the proper difficulty requirement.

On the *balance beam,* new gymnasts make numerous falls, tend to turn in a flat-footed performance, keep their eyes down, and will often be faulted for lack of rhythm or grace. Elite performers, on the other hand, are more prone to the kind of mental mistakes that lead to wobbles; it is also not uncommon for them to fail to meet the difficulty requirement.

In *vaults* beginners have a hard time developing enough speed on the run-up. They also tend to hesitate on the spring board. Both of these miscalculations can result in poor height or distance; can cause the feet or legs to touch the horse; can lead to poor repulsion off the hands; and can cause a poor landing. More experienced gymnasts are frequently given deductions for incorrect body position or for failing to perform the exact movements that were promised.

Inexperienced boys on the *pommel horse* will rest or lean on the apparatus and perform with bent arms or legs. These errors can also be committed by more experienced gymnasts, who also will be faulted for the most common failing on the pommel:

interrupting the smooth swinging motion. The most important aspect of this exercise is that all the movements must blend together in a continuous swinging motion and the most commonly given deductions are for a break in the motion.

On the *still rings*, youngsters just starting out and more experienced athletes have the most trouble keeping the rings still, maintaining good height in their swings, and making a good, steady landing—"sticking" when they land, as it's called.

Deductions

The Federation of International Gymnastics does provide a schedule of deductions for the evaluation of form. For instance, if a gymnast does not appear during a movement to have extended to their full height at the appropriate time, the judge may deduct .1–.2 for a "slight" lack of height, .3–.5 for a "moderate," or .6 or more for a "complete" lack of height. Obviously, at least the first two categories require subjective appraisals.

The first group of deductions illustrated below is confined to movements made by the gymnast. Following these are the deductions that judges can make for the behavior of the gymnast or of the coach. Both types are nonspecific deductions, which means they can be made against any exercise that has a particular element in common. For instance, various exercises include flight elements and swing elements, so the common deductions for these skills are not limited to one event.

This sample of deductions is by no means a complete list. Each specific event also has a list of deductions specific to just one or two events. There are certain errors that are only deducted on the beam, for instance, since there are specific movements that only take place on the beam. The complete list of specific deductions is beyond the scope of this book—but judges and serious competitive gymnasts must be familiar with such deductions. The official tables of general deductions, which apply to many events, are reprinted in the back of this book.

For all of these errors the judges will make deductions ranging from .1 to .5 points.

I. STYLISTIC AND TECHNICAL DEDUCTIONS

These first deductions are made for stylistic or technical errors made by the gymnast during the course of the exercise.

The posture or the position of the legs, arms, feet, body, or head are slightly incorrect. Examples would be lack of toe point, slightly flexed/relaxed knees, poor posture, or head tilted forward.

A greater fault in the position of the legs, arms, feet, body, or head results in a greater deduction.

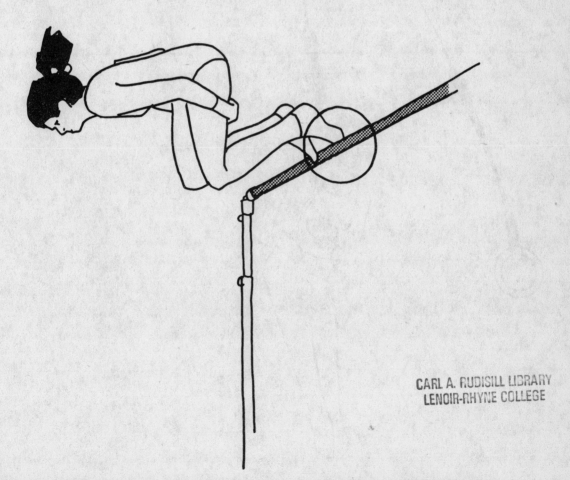

This gymnast has lightly touched the apparatus, in this case the uneven parallel bars, when no touch should have taken place. Touching the floor in a similar manner is also an error.

For a moderate touch of the apparatus—or floor—
the judge should make a bigger deduction.

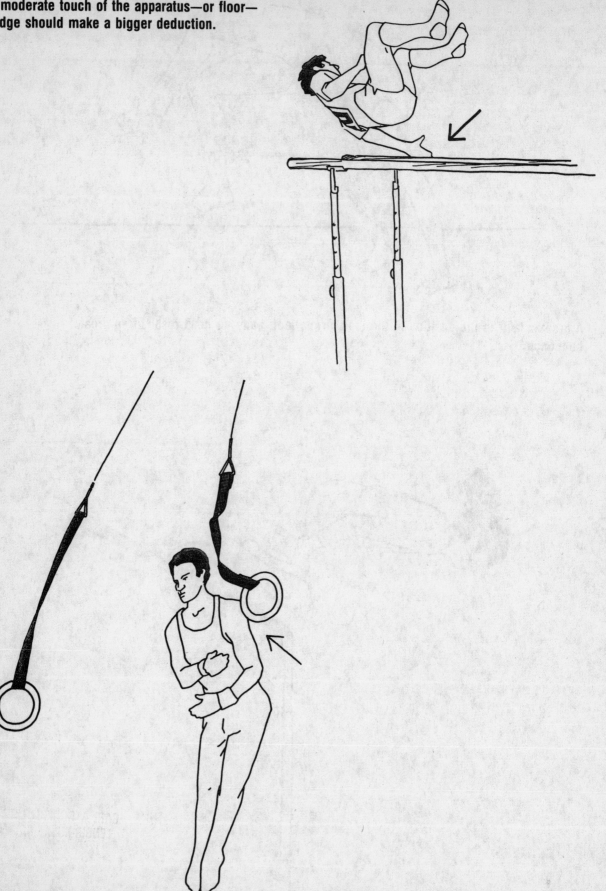

Note: On the rings, it's a judgment call. Did the ring hit the performer, or did the performer hit the ring?

A fault occurs when a performer pauses for preparation, in the midst of movement, for longer than 2 seconds. A judge will make a deduction for each time a pause occurs.

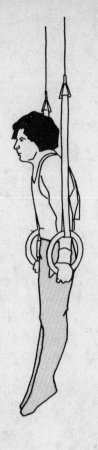

This gymnast has suffered a slight loss of balance, obvious in her unsure landing. A related deduction would be an off-balance step or hop. Any of these will cost a .1 to .2 deduction.

When gymnasts lose control and must briefly support themselves by one or both hands or the floor or apparatus, in this case the parallel bars, that's an error with a standard deduction of .5.

More of a loss of balance (moderate) has been experienced here, as the gymnast has taken 2 (or more) off-balance steps. A similar deduction would be made if the gymnast made a moderately unsure landing, or if he made an additional body movement as he landed to compensate for a loss of balance. The penalty will be a deduction of .3 or .4.

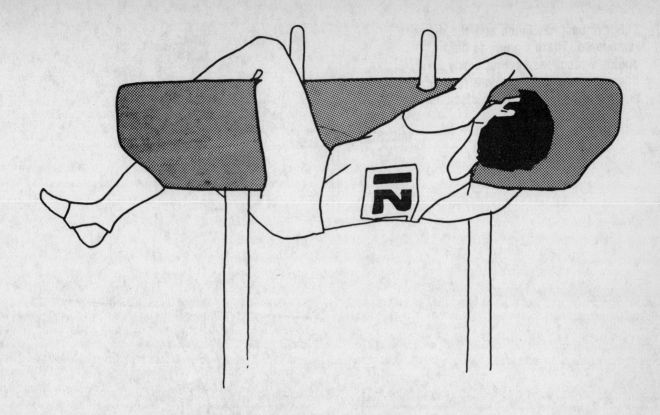

Here the gymnast has very definitely been forced to support himself by both hands. The same deduction is made for a fall on the hips, knees, or against the floor or apparatus. These are going to be costly deductions—the maximum of .5.

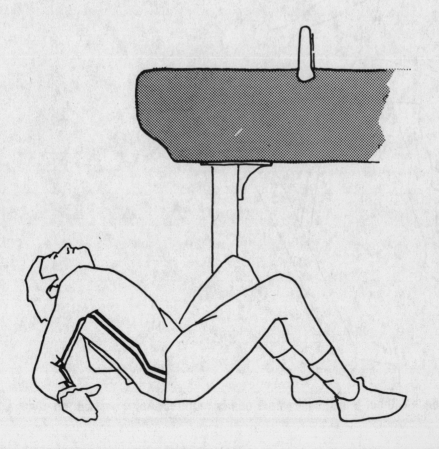

This gymnast has fallen and she never
remounted. There's going to be a
double deduction. Another costly error,
this one costs .5 for the fall, plus an
additional deduction for no dismount.

If the gymnast ends without a dismount where one is required, he or she will be given a
deduction.

The error committed by this gymnast is called an intermediate swing. That is, he made an extra, unnecessary swing in the routine.

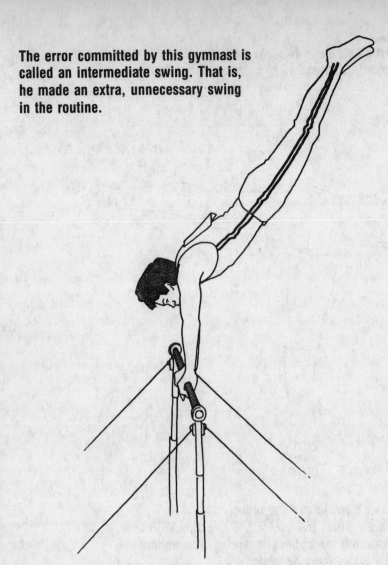

Deductions are also made when, during the course of an event, the gymnast fails to include the required number of parts of various difficulty values (A, B, and C). As discussed earlier, the number of movements of various difficulties depends on the level of the gymnast. However, no matter what the level, the gymnast will lose points on this scale. The greater the difficulty of the omitted part, the greater the deduction.

The gymnast receives a deduction if the routine is either too long or too short.

Another way of losing points is to show too little amplitude in some portion—a "moderate" portion—of the exercise. Amplitude is the amount of extension of all parts of the body—height and the reach of the arms and legs.

Showing a lack of amplitude throughout an exercise also costs a deduction.

A deduction might also be given if a gymnast repeats the use of a connection with the compulsory mount or dismount or an element during the optional exercise. The optional routine must be significantly different from the compulsory exercises.

II. GYMNAST'S BEHAVIOR

Judges give the deductions in the following group for misconduct or errors connected to the performance but not an actual part of the exercise.

Gymnasts are required to make a presentation to the head judge (before commencing the exercise). If they fail to do this, they'll be given a deduction.

A gymnast can also be given a deduction for wearing inappropriate or incorrect attire.

Having no starting number also earns a deduction.

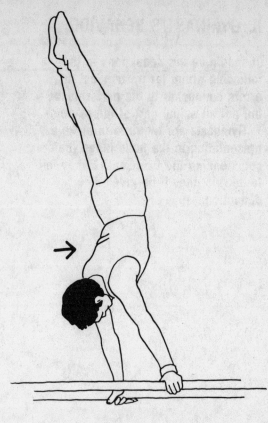

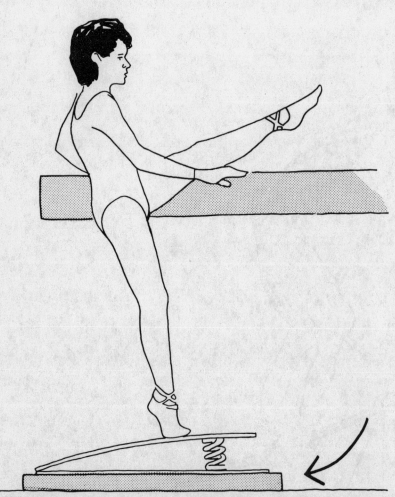

Take-off boards are allowed to be placed on no more than 12 cm (approximately 4¾ inches) thickness of mats. A deduction will be made for a greater thickness.

Gymnasts should start their routines within 30 seconds of the signal. If they take longer than that to start, they earn a deduction.

Elite and Olympic gymnasts should never leave the competition area without the permission of the head judge. If they do, it will cost them.

In the U.S., a gymnast is signalled to begin by the wave of a green flag from the head judge. If a gymnast starts before the signal, there's no deduction, but the exercise is not valid.

Also, the judges have the power to disqualify a gymnast who delays or interrupts the competition.

III. COACH'S BEHAVIOR

Coaches, too, can cost their gymnasts points.

Except to remove the springboard, coaches should not come onto the podium (podiums are used for national competitions)—it'll earn them the maximum .5 deduction.

Coaches should not assist a gymnast during the exercise or landing. Because of the double deduction for assisting and for coming onto the podium (in national competitions) this is a costly action. They can get .5 for presence on podium and .5 for aiding the gymnast.

A coach should not signal a gymnast during the exercise.

The coach also should not touch the gymnast's apparatus. Where applicable, this can earn a double deduction for presence on the podium and for the actual touching.

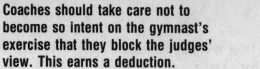

Coaches should take care not to become so intent on the gymnast's exercise that they block the judges' view. This earns a deduction.

Finally—this does not actually pertain to coaches—the jury can decide to give the gymnast a deduction for receiving signs from the spectators.

THE GYMNAST'S FINAL SCORE

During a competitive performance, points are subtracted and a total score determined by each judge. Major competitions will have four judges and a superior judge, while smaller meets will usually have two, although this may vary. The judges pass their scores to the head judge, who makes sure they are relatively close to each other. Exactly how far apart they may range is defined in the rules. If there are four judges the highest and lowest scores are thrown out. The two remaining scores are averaged for the final score. When there are two judges, their scores for the performance are averaged and the resulting figure is the final score. The two scores must still be within range.

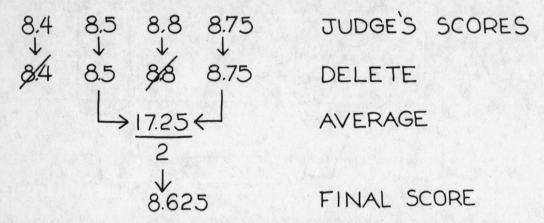

No matter how many judges, there occasionally are ties between competitors. These are not contested; that is, there may be two first-place winners. In age group competitions the awards for ties are presented in order of highest all-around score. If two competitors tie in all-around scores, the winner will be the person who had the single highest score of the competition.

Obviously, unlike judges and referees in other sports, gymnastics judges are not present simply to ensure that the rules are followed, but are there to rate the performances for technical ability, originality, and virtuosity. They not only affect the outcome of a single meet by the way they award points, but as they make decisions and critique performances, they also contribute to the evolution of gymnastic technique. For instance, if a very slight variation on a skill in one performer is seen by other gymnasts to receive a more positive decision by judges, the other gymnasts are likely to adopt that variation.

The arena of judging in competitive gymnastics has long been a source of controversy. In international gymnastics there have been instances where judges have been suspected of making decisions biased toward their home countries' teams.

In U.S. competitions in the past, because of the largely volunteer nature of many gymnastics meets, the standard of knowledge and training among judges varied dramatically, sometimes with a poor effect on the involved gymnastics programs. Only relatively recently has a pool of competent, professional gymnastics judges been developed at all levels of gymnastics meets in the U.S.

There are two national judging organizations in the U.S. today: for men (National Gymnastics Judging Association) and for women (National Association of Women's Gymnastics Judges). The testing and training procedures conducted by these organizations are very rigorous; anyone wishing to become a judge must apply to one of these groups and pass its training program.

The role of the judge cannot be overemphasized. He or she carries a great deal of power; deciding winners, ranks, and championships. Judges not only must know the rules of the sport thoroughly, but they also must keep up to date on the changing composition of the events and be able to be fair and unbiased. They must know the difficulty levels of all A, B, and C skills; they must know how much to deduct for mistakes; they must be able to spot errors quickly and make the correct deduction while continuing to observe the ongoing performance.

EXCERPTS FROM THE UNITED STATES GYMNASTICS FEDERATION 1988–1992

Excerpts of rules reprinted with permission from the United States Gymnastics Federation, Pan American Plaza, Suite 300, 210 S. Capitol Avenue, Indianapolis, IN 46225. Rules excerpted from the Junior USGF Olympic Compulsories 1989–1992 (Women's Gymnastics) and the USGF Junior Olympic Compulsories 1988–1992 (Artistic Gymnastics).

Women's Gymnastics

GENERAL FAULTS AND PENALTIES—

Uneven Bars, Balance Beam, Floor Exercise and Dance

It is intended that all elements and connections be performed with maximum amplitude and execution. Any departure from the correct technique of performance will be penalized according to the Table of Faults following small, medium and large errors. Deduct all execution errors leading to a fall. No single element may be reversed unless otherwise stated. Deductions MAY exceed the value of the element. General deductions apply when specific deductions are not listed.

DEDUCTION

I. CHANGES IN PRESCRIBED TEXT —

*1. Changing, reversing or omitting a small part	.10
2. Changing, reversing or omitting a series of connections	.30
3. Changing or omitting a major element	.50 + value
4. Reversing a major element	.30
5. Failure to complete a major element	up to the value
6. Incorrect position of arms, head or feet —	
Deduct in general (not each time) according to small, medium or large errors	up to .40

*Changing — performing a different element than the element prescribed.
  (does NOT include body position failures in Saltos)
Omitting — leaving the element out completely.

II. RHYTHM —

1. Lack of continuity in connections	.10
2. Improper rhythm during major element	up to .20
3. For overall rhythm during exercise —	
Deduct in general for small or medium errors	up to .40
4. Pauses (more than 2 seconds) before or after elements	.10

Balance Beam and Floor Exercise —

1. Change in prescribed rhythm of connections when specifically noted in text	.10
2. Undertime or overtime	.20
3. BB — lack of continuity in acrobatics series	up to .30
lack of continuity in gymnastics series	up to .20
4. FX — lack of continuity in series of acrobatics or gymnastics	up to .20

III. DIRECTION AND PLACEMENT OF ELEMENTS —

Balance Beam and Floor Exercise —

1. Small error in line of direction or spacing	.10
2. Error in line of direction of acrobatic or gymnastics series	.20
3. Error in line of direction of placement of whole section of floor pattern	.30

IV. EXECUTION —

1. Bent arms or knees	up to	.30
2. Leg separation	up to	.20
3. Balance errors — small, medium, large	up to	.40
4. Fall		.50
5. Incorrect body alignment, position or posture	up to	.20
6. Lack of coordination on connections		.10
7. Lack of lightness		.10
8. Movement lacking quality and maturity (General deduction for whole routine)	up to	.30

Uneven Bars —

1. Feet contacting floor	slightly		.10
	moderately	up to	.30
	full weight		.50
2. Alternate hand grasp of bar			.20
3. Regaining hand grasp without supplementary support			.30
4. Using supplementary support to regain position (foot against uprights, knee swing up)			.50
5. Extra swing			.30
6. Taking more than one step and closing feet on glide mounts			.20

Balance Beam, Floor Exercise and Dance —

1. Insufficient split	up to	.20
2. Incorrect leg position	up to	.20
3. Failure to contract or extend	each	.10
4. Degree of turn not exact (360° or more)	up to	.30
5. Hand placement incorrect during acrobatics	up to	.20
6. Lack of coordination on supple body movements and waves		.10

V. AMPLITUDE —

Uneven Bars —

1. Lacking internal body amplitude during extended positions	up to	.20
2. Insufficient external amplitude away from bar during swinging and circling movements	up to	.20

Balance Beam, Floor Exercise, and Dance —

1. Insufficient amplitude on connection		.10
2. Steps not on balls of feet where indicated (General Deduction for whole routine)	up to	.20
3. Turns not on ball of foot	each up to	.20

VI. LANDING —

1. Landing heavy and uncertain (any body movement)		.10
2. Taking one full step after landing		.10
3. Taking two full steps after landing		.20
4. Taking more than two full steps after landing		.30
5. Deep squat or pike upon landing		.30
6. TOUCHING the apparatus or the floor	up to	.30
7. SUPPORT of one or both hands		.50
8. Fall on the hips, knees, on or against the apparatus		.50

Vault-Levels 5, 6, 7
Handspring

Levels 5 & 6: Horse height is optional. NOT to exceed 120 cm.
Level 7: Horse height regulation for Age Group.

Jump from the board with a stretched body to an inverted position on the horse.   Push off from the horse and land in demi-plié and then extend.

Table of Penalties

A.	**First Flight:**				
	1.	Insufficient flight from board to horse		up to	.50
	2.	Body bent during flight - piked or arched		up to	.30
	3.	Legs bent, straddled or opened	(each)	up to	.30
	4.	Strong tuck of legs		up to	.50
	5.	Poor direction			.10
B.	**Support Phase:**				
	1.	Using force to establish support		up to	.50
	2.	Incorrect alignment (arched, piked, shoulders forward of hands)	(each)	up to	.20
	3.	Arms bent up to 90°		up to	1.00
	4.	Lack of repulsion		up to	1.00
	5.	Alternate repulsion of hands		up to	.30
C.	**Second Flight:**				
	1.	Insufficient height		up to	.50
	2.	Insufficient length		up to	.50
	3.	Body bent during flight - piked or arched		up to	.30
	4.	Legs bent, straddled or opened	(each)	up to	.30
	5.	Poor body alignment		up to	.20
D.	**Landing:**				
	1.	Landing heavy and uncertain (any body movement)			.10
	2.	Taking one full step after landing			.10
	3.	Taking two full steps after landing			.20
	4.	Taking more than two full steps after landing			.30
	5.	Deep squat or pike upon landing			.30
	6.	Touch of body against apparatus			.30
	7.	Touch of one or both hands on the floor upon landing			.30
	8.	Support of both hands on floor			.50
	9.	Falling on the knees, hips or out of balance with support against the apparatus			.50
E.	**General:**				
	1.	Poor direction of the vault		up to	.30
	2.	Lack of dynamics (speed & force)		up to	.20
F.	**Coaching or Spotting Deductions:**				
	1.	Coach between board and horse			.50
	2.	Aid of coach during first flight			Void
	3.	Aid of coach during second flight			Void
	4.	Aid of coach during landing			.50
	5.	Coach giving signs, talking, touching apparatus or blocking view of the judges			.20

Vault-Level 10

Yamashita

Jump to an inverted support on the horse.   In the second flight, pike and extend the body before landing. Land in demi-plié then extend.

Table of Penalties

A. **First Flight:**

1.	Body bent during flight (piked or arched)	up to	.30
2.	Legs bent, straddle or opened	(each) up to	.30
3.	Strong tuck of legs	up to	.50
4.	Poor direction		.10

B. **Support Phase:**

1.	Incorrect alignment, (arched, piked, shoulders forward of hands)	(each) up to	.20
2.	Late repulsion	up to	1.00
3.	Arms bent in support	up to	1.00

C. **Second Flight:**

1.	Insufficient height	up to	.50
2.	Insufficient distance	up to	.50
3.	Insufficient hip angle (greater than 90°)	up to	.30
4.	Hip angle greater than 135°		**Void**
5.	Failure to extend by horizontal	up to	.30
6.	Failure to stretch before landing	up to	.20

D. **Landing:**

1.	Landing heavy and uncertain (any body movement)	.10
2.	Taking one full step after landing	.10
3.	Taking two full steps after landing	.20
4.	Taking more than two full steps after landing	.30
5.	Deep squat or pike upon landing	.30
6.	Touch of body against apparatus	.30
7.	Touch of one or both hands on the floor upon landing	.30
8.	Support of both hands on floor	.50
9.	Falling on the knees, hips or out of balance with support against the apparatus	.50

E. **General:**

1.	Poor direction of vault	up to	.30
2.	Lack of dynamics (speed and force)	up to	.20

F. **Coaching and Spotting Deductions:**

1.	Coach between board and horse	.50
2.	Aid of coach during first flight	**Void**
3.	Aid of coach during second flight	**Void**
4.	Aid of coach during landing	.50
5.	Coach giving signs, talking, touching apparatus or blocking view of the judges	.20

Vaulting—Summary Skill Sheet

LEVEL I Skills

1 Running Speed

Board Drills to a Landing Mat:

2 Straight Jump
3 Tuck Jump
4 Straddle Jump
5 Jump 180° Turn

LEVEL II Skills

1 Running Speed

Squat onto Horse and. . .

2 Straight Jump
3 Tuck Jump
4 Straddle Jump
5 Jump 180° Turn

LEVEL III -
1 Running speed
2 Front Handspring to 2 foot

LEVEL IV -
1 Squat Vault

LEVEL 5 (Bronze)

Handspring
(Horse height optional - Not to exceed 120 cm.)

LEVEL 6 (Silver)

Handspring

LEVEL 7 (Gold)

Handspring
(Regulation height for age group)

LEVEL 10

Yamashita

Uneven Bars-Skill Summary Sheet

LEVEL I Skills

1 Back Pullover
2 Cast to Horizontal and return to suport
3 Stride Circle Forward
4 Back Hip Circle
5 Single Leg squat through
6 Counter Swing
7 Underswing Dismount

LEVEL III Skills

1 Run Out Single Leg Kip
2 Glide Swing

3 Long Hang Kip
4 Long Hang Pull over HB
5 Basket Swing
6 Front Hip Circle Cast
7 Straddle Sole Circle Dismount

LEVEL II - Sequence using Level I skills

LEVEL IV - Sequence using Level III skills

LEVEL 5 (Bronze)	LEVEL 6 (Silver)	LEVEL 7 (Gold)	LEVEL 10
Straddle Glide Kip	Glide Kip	Glide Kip	Pendle Kip
Front Hip Circle	Cast 30°	Cast 60°	*Cast Hsd. 180° tur
Squat on Low Bar	*Clear Hip Circle 30°	*Clear Hip Circle 60°	*3/4 Giant Circle 180° Turn
Long Hang Pullover HB	Std. Glide, Back Kip	Std. Glide, Back Kip	*Underswing 180° Turn
Underswing	Long Hang Kip	Long Hang Kip	Std. Glide Back Kip
Counter Swing to Straddle Stand on LB	Front Hip Circle	Cast 60°	Long Hang Kip
*Straddle Sole Circle Dismount	Cast 30°	*Flyaway Stretched	Cast Handstand
	*Flyaway Tucked (or) Flyaway Stretched		*Clear Hip Circle H
			*Flyaway Stretched

All elements .40
except * = .60

Balance Beam—Summary Skill Sheet

LEVEL I Skills

1 Walk forward, backward, sideward (in relevé)
2 Chasse R - L
3 Waltz pattern
4 Step hop finish demi-plié
5 Relevé Turns

6 Stretched Jump
7 Arabesque (Hold 2 Sec. 45°)
8 1 Foot sit to "V" sit
9 Forward Roll
10 Stretched Jump Dismount

LEVEL III Skills

1 Walk Forward with knee lift & kick above horizontal
2 Body Wave
3 Arabesque hop (rear leg 45°)
4 Scale
5 180° - 180° Turn (same direction)

6 Stretched Jump Forward
7 Split Leap 120°
8 Backward Roll
9 Cartwheel
10 Round Off Dismount

LEVEL II - Sequence using Level I skills

LEVEL IV - Sequence using Level III skills

LEVEL 5 (Bronze)	LEVEL 6 (Silver)	LEVEL 7 (Gold)	LEVEL 10
*Squat on Mount	*Oblique run on Mount	*Free jump to 2 feet	*Press Handstand
Backward Swing Turn	Forward Swing Turn	180° Passé	Cartwheel, *Flic Flac, Sissone
Body Wave	Body Wave	Body Wave	Scale (Demi-plié)
*Cross Handstand	Back Walkover	*Flic Flac	Stretched Jump forward (arched)
Split Leap, Stretched Jump Forward	Stag-Split Leap, Stretched Jump Forward	Split Leap Hitch Kick,	Back Walkover
Cartwheel	*Cartwheel Handstand Straddle down	*Cross Handstand, Back Walkover	Split Leap, 360° Turn
Assemblé	Assemblé, Stretched Jump	Assemblé, Stretched Jump 180° Turn	Scale (diagonal)
360° Turn	360° Turn	360° Turn	Round Off * Back Salto Stretched
Scale	Scale	Scale	
*Round Off	*Brani	Cartwheel, *Back Salto Tucked	

All elements .40
except * (.60)

Floor Exercise—Summary Skill Sheet

LEVEL I Skills

1 Forward roll
2 Handstand (hold 1 second)
3 Handstand Forward roll

4 Backward roll
5 Back extension roll (bent arms)
6 Cartwheel Right
7 Cartwheel Left
8 Hurdle Cartwheel
9 Round Off
10 Back Walkover

LEVEL II - Sequence using Level I skills

LEVEL III Skills

1 Pike dive forward roll
2 Handstand switch legs
3 Cartwheel to Handstand, press down to straddle stand
4 Handstand 180° turn
5 Dive Cartwheel
6 Back extension roll (straight arms)
7 Front Walkover
8 Headspring to 2 feet off folded mat
9 Front Handspring step out
10 Flic Flac rebound

LEVEL IV - Sequence using Level III skills

LEVEL 5 (Bronze)	LEVEL 6 (Silver)	LEVEL 7 (Gold)	LEVEL 10
Body Wave	Body Wave	Body Wave	Round Off, Flic Flac, *Back Salto
Dive Cartwheel	Aerial Cartwheel	*Front salto, Forward roll	Back Extension Roll
Round Off, Flic Flac, Flic Flac Step Out	Round Off, Flic Flac, Flic Flac, *Back Salto Tucked	Round Off, Flic Flac, *Back Salto Stretched	360° Turn
360° Turn (outward *passé*)	360° Turn (Front *Attitude*)	540° Turn	Valdez
Back Walkover	Back Walkover Switch Legs	Handstand 180° Pirouette Back Walkover	Switch Leap
	Split Leap	Stag-split Leap, Side Leap	360° Stretched Jump
Fouette	*Tour jeté*	*Tour jeté*	
Ft Handspring, Round Off, Back Extension roll	Ft Handspring, Round Off, Flic Flac	Ft Handspring, Round Off, Flic Flac, * Back Salto Tucked	Aerial Cartwheel, Flic Fla *Back Salto Stretched
Hitch Kick, Handstand Forward roll	Hitch Kick, Front Walkover	Hitch Kick, Aerial Cartwheel	*Jeté en Tournant*
			Round Off, Flic Flac, *Arabian Salto Tucked Tinsica
All elements .40 except * (.60)			360° Turn

Dance—Summary Skill Sheet

LEVEL I Skills

1 Five Positions of Feet
2 Five Positions of Arms
3 *Sous-Sus*
4 *Demi-plié*
5 *Battment Tendu Simple*
6 *Rond de Jambe a'Terre*
7 *Relevé*
8 *Temp Levé*
9 *Changement*
10 *Echappé*

LEVEL III Skills

1 *Grand Plié*
2 *Battement Fondu*
3 *Devleoppé*
4 *Grand Battement*
5 Splits
6 *Jeté Ordinaire*
7 *Glissade*
8 *Assemblé*
9 *Pas de Bourrée*
10 *Sissone*

LEVEL II - Sequence using
Level I skills

LEVEL IV - Sequence using
Level III skills

LEVEL 5 (Bronze)

Épaulement

Petit Temps Lié Right

Petit Temps Lié Left

Attitudes

Soutenu en Tournant

Pirouette en Dehores

Soutenu en Tournant

Pirouette en Dedans

Grand Jeté

Port de Bras

LEVEL 6 (Silver)

Port de Bras

Pas Ballotte

Cabriole

Brisé Fermé

Pas Ballotte

Cabriole

Brisé Fermé

Pas de Bourrée

Entrechat Quatre

Emboite en tournant

Arabesque

Fouetté en Tournant

Torso Swing

Split

LEVEL 7 (Gold)

Tour Chainé

Tour A La Seconde

Sideward Lunge

Curtsey

Pirouette en Dehores

Pas de Basque

Glissade

Pas de Chat

Arabesque

*Tour Jeté en
     Tournant*

Tour en L'Air

Port de Bras

Men's Gymnastics

JUDGING GUIDELINES

As per article 40 of the 1985 F.I.G. Code of Points, the execution and technical aspects of a compulsory exercise are evaluated using the same standards as for the optional exercises. However, in order to help clarify the evaluation of the 1988-1992 Jr. Olympic Age Group Compulsory Routines the following judging guidelines are provided.

Standard Deductions—to be applied to **all** events
1. **Hold parts**
   —All designated "hold" parts should be held **2 seconds.**
   —All designated "momentary hold" parts should be held **1 second.**
   a. Hold parts (2 sec.)
   0.3 deduction for a 1 second hold
   0.5 deduction for no hold
   b. Momentary hold parts (1 sec.)
   0.3 deduction for no hold
   c. A **0.3** deduction should be taken for:
   —holding a part when not called for . . .
   —a 3 second or more hold when a 2 second hold is called for . . .
   —a 2 second or more hold when a momentary hold is called for . . .
2. **Omitted parts**
   —**Deduct the full value** of the part
3. **Added parts** (including extra circles on Pommel Horse and extra giants on Horizontal Bar)
   —**0.3** each time only (there is no facilitation deduction)
4. **Partially shown parts** or technical execution that is **extremely** poor
   —Deduct **half the value** of the part, plus general execution errors
5. **Stopping** when not required
   —**0.3** each time
6. **Falls off** the apparatus
   —**0.5** each time
7. **Spotting**
   a. If assistance is needed to complete a skill
   —Deduct the **full value** of the part plus general execution deductions
   b. If spotting contact is made **without** assisting the skill or interrupting the routine
   —Deduct **0.3**
   c. If spotting assistance is made which interrupts the routine but does not help complete the skill
   —Deduct **0.5**
8. **Dismount landing**
   —Deduct **0.2 minimum** for any execution error
   —Deduct **0.3 to 0.5** for hands touching the floor with support, kneeling or falling upon landing

Specific Deductions—to be applied to specific events at **all** levels
Floor Exercise

1. More or less than the required number of steps
   —Deduct **0.3** each time
2. Going out of the area
   —Deduct **0.1** each time
3. Walking in a handstand or extra hand placement during pirouette
   —Deduct **0.1** per step, **up to 0.5** per occurrence
4. Interrupted upward motion in hold or strength parts
   —Deduct **0.3** each time
5. Strength parts executed with swing
   —Deduct **up to 0.3** each time

6. Non-dismount landings—landings that occur prior to the dismount landing
   a. Small steps or hops
      —Deduct **0.1** each time
   b. Several steps or hops or touching hands to the floor without support
      —Deduct **0.2** each time
   c. Hands touching the floor with support, kneeling or falling upon landing
      —Deduct **0.3 to 0.5**

Technical Insufficiencies

1. **Thirty Degree Rule**
   —Deductions of **up to 0.3** for improper body, arm or leg positions each time will be determined by a **30 degree angle** for all elements.
   This will be applied as follows:
   A **10** degree divergence from required position—Deduct **0.1**
   A **20** degree divergence from required position—Deduct **0.2**
   A **30** degree divergence from required position—Deduct **0.3**
   More than a 30 degree divergence—Deduct half the value of the element or 0.3 to 0.5, whichever is more
   As a specific example:
   If straight arms are required on a certain element, if the gymnast bends his arms:
   10 degrees—Deduct 0.1
   20 degrees—Deduct 0.2
   30 degrees—Deduct 0.3
   More than 30 degrees—Deduct half the value or 0.3 to 0.5, whichever is more

2. **Height Insufficiencies**
   —Deductions of **up to 0.3** for insufficient height of tumbling elements shall be taken between head and chest height where a tumbling element that is required to be head height and is performed chest height would receive a **0.3** deduction. If the same element is performed head height there would be no deduction. If the element is performed below chest height, half the value of the element would be deducted, or 0.3 to 0.5, whichever is more.

3. **General Execution/Form**
   —Deductions of **up to 0.3** for improper position of head, feet and hands each time.

4. **Alignment, etc.**
   —Deductions of **up to 0.3** for improper alignment of elements, contact and use of floor when not needed and not involving a stop or fall each time.

5. **Rhythm**
   —Deductions of **up to 0.3** for interrupted flow of individual or combined elements not involving a stop or fall each time.

Pommel Horse

1. Extra swings
   —Deduct **0.3** each time

2. Sitting on the apparatus
   —Deduct **0.5** each time

3. Interrupted upward motion in swing parts
   —Deduct **0.3** each time

4. Swing parts executed with strength
   —Deduct **up to 0.3** each time

Technical Insufficiencies

1. **Thirty Degree Rule**
   —Deductions of **up to 0.3** for failure to maintain the required 60 degree straddle of the legs on single leg and scissor work—Apply 30 Degree Rule as follows:

Performance	Deduction
60 degree straddle	0.0
50 degree straddle	0.1
40 degree straddle	0.2
30 degree straddle	0.3
Less than 30 degree straddle	Half the value or 0.3 to 0.5, whichever is more

—Deductions of **up to 0.3** for failure to maintain a 110 degree body angle during loop and circle work—Apply 30 degree rule as follows:

Performance	Deduction
110 degree body angle	0.0
100 degree body angle	0.1
90 degree body angle	0.2
80 degree body angle	0.3
Less than 80 degree angle	Half the value or 0.3 to 0.5, whichever is more

2. Amplitude Insufficiencies

—Deductions of **up to 0.3** for failure to attain the required amplitude on straddled or stride swings, single leg work or front scissor work will be determined by the following: With a 60 degree straddle and,

Performance	Deduction
Lower leg 15 degrees below horizontal	0.0
Lower leg 25 degrees below horizontal	0.1
Lower leg 35 degrees below horizontal	0.2
Lower leg 45 degrees below horizontal	0.3
Lower leg more than 45 degrees below horizontal	Half the value or 0.3 to 0.5, whichever is more

3. General Execution/Form

—Deductions of **up to 0.3** for improper position of head, feet and hands each time. Also apply 30 Degree Rule to leg form and arm positions.

4. Alignment, etc.

—Deductions of **up to 0.3** for improper alignment of elements, contact and use of floor or pommel horse when not needed and not involving a stop or fall each time.

5. Rhythm

—Deductions of **up to 0.3** for interrupted flow of individual or combined elements not involving a stop or fall each time.

Rings

1. Swinging of cables
   —Deduct **up to 0.3** during each element by applying 30 Degree Rule from vertical cable position.
2. Extra swings
   —Deduct **0.3** each time
3. Interrupted upward motion in swing, hold or strength parts
   —Deduct **0.3** each time
4. Swing parts executed with strength or vice versa
   —Deduct **up to 0.3** each time

Technical Insufficiencies

1. Thirty Degree Rule

—Deductions of **up to 0.3** for failure to attain the required amplitude on elements measurable in degrees for technical insufficiencies—Apply 30 Degree Rule as follows:

A 10 degree divergence from required amplitude—Deduct 0.1
A 20 degree divergence from required amplitude—Deduct 0.2
A 30 degree divergence from required amplitude—Deduct 0.3
More than a 30 degree divergence—Deduct half the value of the element or 0.3 to 0.5, whichever is more

As a specific example:

If an element is required to be performed at a 45 degree angle above horizontal Apply 30 Degree Rule as follows:

Performance	Deduction
To 45 degrees above horizontal	0.0
To 35 degrees above horizontal	0.1
To 25 degrees above horizontal	0.2
To 15 degrees above horizontal	0.3
Below 15 degrees above horizontal	Half the value or 0.3 to 0.5, whichever is more

2. General Execution/Form

—Deductions of **up to 0.3** for improper position of head, feet and hands each time. Also apply 30 Degree Rule to leg form and arm and body positions.

3. Alignment, etc.

—Deductions of **up to 0.3** for improper alignment of elements, contact and use of rings when not needed and not involving a stop or fall each time.

4. Rhythm

—Deductions of **up to 0.3** for interrupted flow of individual or combined elements not involving a stop or fall each time.

Vaulting—See description at each level.

Parallel Bars

1. Walking in a handstand
   —Deduct **0.1** per step, **up to 0.5** per occurrence

2. Extra swings
   —Deduct **0.3** each time

3. Sitting on the apparatus
   —Deduct **0.5** each time

4. Interrupted upward motion in swing, hold or strength parts
   —Deduct **0.3** each time

5. Swing parts executed with strength or vice versa
   —Deduct **up to 0.3** each time

Technical Insufficiencies

1. Thirty Degree Rule

—Deductions of **up to 0.3** for failure to attain the required amplitude on elements measurable in degrees for technical insufficiencies—Apply 30 Degree Rule as follows:

A 10 degree divergence from required amplitude—Deduct 0.1

A 20 degree divergence from required amplitude—Deduct 0.2

A 30 degree divergence from required amplitude—Deduct 0.3

More than a 30 degree divergence—Deduct half the value of the element or 0.3 to 0.5, whichever is more

As a specific example:

If an element is required to be performed at a 30 degree angle above horizontal Apply 30 Degree Rule as follows:

Performance	Deduction
To 30 degrees above horizontal	0.0
To 20 degrees above horizontal	0.1
To 10 degrees above horizontal	0.2
To horizontal	0.3
To below horizontal	Half the value or 0.3 to 0.5, whichever is more

2. General Execution/Form

—Deductions of **up to 0.3** for improper position of head, feet and hands each time. Also apply 30 Degree Rule to leg form and arm and body positions.

3. Alignment, etc.

—Deductions of **up to 0.3** for improper alignment of elements, contact and use of bars when not needed and not involving a stop or fall each time.

4. Rhythm

—Deductions of **up to 0.3** for interrupted flow of individual or combined elements not involving a stop or fall each time.

Horizontal Bar

1. Extra swings
   —Deduct **0.3** each time

2. Interrupted upward motion in swing parts
—Deduct **0.3** each time
3. Swing parts executed with strength
—Deduct **up to 0.3** each time
4. Lack of required spotter
—Deduct **0.5** without warning

Technical Insufficiencies

1. **Thirty Degree Rule**
—Deductions of **up to 0.3** for failure to attain the required amplitude on elements measurable in degrees for technical insufficiencies—Apply 30 Degree Rule as follows:

> A 10 degree divergence from required amplitude—Deduct 0.1
> A 20 degree divergence from required amplitude—Deduct 0.2
> A 30 degree divergence from required amplitude—Deduct 0.3
> More than a 30 degree divergence—Deduct half the value of the element or 0.3 to 0.5, whichever is more

As a specific example:

> If an element is required to be performed at horizontal Apply 30 Degree Rule as follows:

Performance	Deduction
To horizontal	0.0
To 10 degrees below horizontal	0.1
To 20 degrees below horizontal	0.2
To 30 degrees below horizontal	0.3
To below 30 degrees below horizontal	Half the value or 0.3 to 0.5, whichever is more

2. **General Execution/Form**
—Deductions of **up to 0.3** for improper position of head, feet and hands each time. Also apply 30 Degree Rule to leg form and arm and body positions.

3. **Alignment, etc.**
—Deductions of **up to 0.3** for improper alignment of elements, contact and use of horizontal bar when not needed and not involving a stop or fall each time.

4. **Rhythm**
—Deductions of **up to 0.3** for interrupted flow of individual or combined elements not involving a stop or fall each time.

LEVEL I

Floor Exercise

Designated Virtuous Elements (each worth **0.1**)

1. Tucked front somersault in part 1. well above head height
2. Stretched dive roll in part 1. head height
3. Layout back somersault in part 4. well above head height
4. Straddle jump in part 8. head height
5. Front scale in part 9. with back leg 45 degrees above horizontal
6. Full twisting layout back somersault in part 10. well above head height.

Major elements summary

Tucked front step out, front handspring
Two foot front handspring, dive roll
Swedish fall, 2½ double leg circles
Round off, flip flop, flip flop, layout back
Reverse pirouette, roll forward to splits
Stiff-stiff press
Straddle jump, punch front, headspring
Cartwheel, forward lunge, front scale
Round off, flip flop, full

Pommel Horse

Designated Virtuous Elements (0.1 each time **up to 0.6**)

1. Body extended throughout loops and/or circles (body angle of 135 degrees or more)
2. Ninety degree or greater straddle maintained in single leg work and/or scissor work
3. Flank dismount in part 10. above 45 degrees above horizontal

Major elements summary

Loop
Flair loop
Single leg back stockli
Reverse scissor
False scissor backward
Front scissor to front pick up
Direct stockli B
Kehre in
Stockli backward to flank dismount

Rings

Designated Virtuous Elements (each worth **0.1, up to 0.6** total)

1. Back kip to handstand, no hold in part 1.
2. Cross in part 2. held 2 seconds
3. Straight body inlocate in part 4. through handstand
4. Back uprise in part 5. to handstand
5. Straight arm back uprise to handstand in part 7.
6. High dislocate in part 9. through handstand
7. Tucked double back dismount in part 10. with body extended at ring height

Vault

Virtuosity

Up to 0.2 for post-flight distance
Up to 0.2 for post-flight height

*Notes

Height Requirement: The hips of the gymnast must rise 1½ meters at the peak of flight and after contact with the horse to receive no height deduction. Showing extreme height could be awarded **up to 0.2** virtuosity.

Distance Requirements: Marks shall be placed on the landing mat at the following distances: 1, 1½, 2, and 2½ meters from the horse. Corresponding deductions/virtuosity shall be as follows:

If the gymnast lands between:	
0 and 1 meter from the horse	0.5 deduction
1 and 1½ meters	0.3 deduction
1½ and 2 meters	0 deduction
2 and 2½ meters	+0.1 bonus
over 2½ meters	+0.2 bonus

Landing: The minimum landing deduction is **0.2**. This means that any landing that is not "stuck" would receive **at least** a 0.2 deduction.

Parallel Bars

Designated Virtuous Elements (up to 0.6 total)

1. Peach basket in partl. with straight arms to 30 degrees above horizontal—0.1
2. Peach basket in part 1. with straight arms to 60 degrees above horizontal—0.2
3. Front uprise in part 2. with hips shoulder height—0.1
4. Reverse stutz in part 3. with body horizontal at the end of the turn—0.1
5. Reverse stutz in part 3. with body above 30 degrees at the end of the turn—0.2
6. Layout back somersault in part 10. with exceptional height—0.1

Horizontal Bar

Designated Virtuous Elements (each worth 0.1, up to 0.6 total)

1. Stem rise in part 1. with turn completed at 45 degrees above horizontal
2. Swing forward in part 2. to nominal handstand
3. Stoop through in part 4. from a nominal handstand
4. Dislocate in part 4. to 60 degrees above horizontal at extension of the body
5. Hop to over grips in part 5. to nominal handstand
6. Layout flyaway in part 10. performed with exceptional height

LEVEL II

Floor Exercise

Designated Virtuous Elements (each worth 0.1)

1. Layout back somersault in part 1. well above head height
2. Front somersault in part 4. head height
3. Each leg on hitch kick in part 5. going 45 degrees above horizontal
4. Front scale in part 6. with back leg 45 degrees above horizontal
5. Pancake in part 8. with chest flat on the floor and at least a 160 degree straddle of the legs
6. Straight arm back extension roll in part 9.
7. Tucked back somersault in part 10. well above head height

Major elements summary

Round off, flip flop, flip flop, layout back
Prone fall, one double leg circle
Straddled press to handstand
Front handspring, front, headspring
Hitch kick, turn, front scale
Front handspring, 2 foot handspring, dive roll
Pancake, back extension roll
Round off, flip flop, tucked back

Pommel Horse

Designated Virtuous Elements (0.1 each time up to 0.6)

1. Body extended throughout loops and/or circles (body angle of 135 degrees or more)
2. Ninety degree or greater straddle maintained in single leg work and/or scissor work

Major elements summary

Loop
Loop around
Single leg back stockli
Reverse scissor
Front scissor
Front pick up to circles
Flair circles
Direct stockli B dismount (Back moore down)

Rings

Designated Virtuous Elements (each worth **0.1, up to 0.6** total)

1. Inlocate in part 2. with shoulders well above ring height
2. High inlocate in part 3. through handstand
3. Back uprise in part 4. to 45 degrees above horizontal
4. Straddled press in part 6. with straight arms
5. Back uprise in part 7. to 45 degrees above horizontal
6. High dislocate in part 9. through handstand
7. Layout flyaway in part 10. with shoulders well above ring height at release

Vault

Height Requirement: The hips of the gymnast must rise 1½ meters at the peak of flight and after contact with the horse to receive no height deduction. Showing extreme height could be awarded **up to 0.2** virtuousity.

Distance Requirements: Marks shall be placed on the landing mat at the following distances: 1, 1½, 2, and 2½ meters from the horse. Corresponding deductions/virtuosity shall be as follows:

If the gymnast lands between:	
0 and 1 meter from the horse	0.5 deduction
1 and 1½ meters	0.3 deduction
1½ and 2 meters	0 deduction
2 and 2½ meters	+0.1 bonus
over 2½ meters	+0.2 bonus

Landing: The minimum landing deduction is **0.2**. This means that any landing that is not "stuck" would receive **at least** a 0.2 deduction.

Parallel Bars

Designated Virtuous Elements (up to 0.6 total)

1. Peach basket in part 1. with straight arms to horizontal—0.1
2. Peach basket in part 1. with straight arms to 30 degrees above horizontal—0.2
3. Stutz in part 4. to nominal handstand—0.1
4. Early drop to cast in part 5.
5. Back uprise in part 6. to 30 degrees above horizontal—0.1
6. Giant glide kip to support in part 7.—0.1
7. Tucked back somersault in part 10. with exceptional height—0.1

Horizontal Bar

Designated Virtuous Elements (each worth **0.1, up to 0.6** total)

1. Cast forward in part 1. to 45 degrees above horizontal
2. Back uprise in part 2. to nominal handstand
3. Free hip circle in part 3. to nominal handstand
4. Straddled toe on in part 4. using a late drop to the toe on
5. Early turn to the pirouette in part 8.
6. Tuck-open flyaway in part 10. with hips well above bar height

LEVEL III

Floor Exercise

Designated Virtuous Elements (each worth 0.1)

1. Tucked back somersault in part 1. above head height
2. Straight arm, straddled press to handstand in part 3. held 2 seconds
3. Side scale in part 6. with at least a 135 degree straddle of the legs
4. Back walkover in part 9. with at least a 180 split of the legs
5. Exceptional height on the stretched rebound in part 10.

Major elements summary

Round off, flip flop, tucked back
Swedish fall, turn to splits
Straight arm, straddled press
Flip flop, flip flop, punch half turn
Cartwheel, side lunge, side scale
Front handspring, 2 foot handspring, 2 foot handspring
Tour jete, back walkover
Front handspring step out, round off, flip flop, flip flop, punch.

Pommel Horse

Designated Virtuous Elements (0.1 each time up to 0.6)

1. Body extended throughout loops and/or circles (body angle of 135 degrees or more)
2. Ninety degree or greater straddle maintained in single leg work and/or scissor work

Major elements summary

Loop
Loop around
Single leg travel up
Undercut, front scissor
Single leg travel down
1½ downhill circles

Rings

Designated Virtuous Elements (each worth 0.1, up to 0.6 total)

1. Pull up in part 1. with straight body
2. Pull out of hang in part 3. with straight body
3. Straight body inlocate in part 4. with shoulder lift
4. Straight body inlocate in part 5. with shoulders at ring height
5. Back uprise in part 6. 45 degrees above horizontal
6. Press in part 7. to handstand, with or without hold
7. High dislocate in part 9. with shoulders well above ring height
8. Layout flyaway in part 10. with shoulders well above ring height at release

Vault

Height Requirement: The hips of the gymnast must rise 1 meter at the peak of flight and after contact with the horse to receive no height deduction. Showing extreme height could be awarded **up to 0.2** virtuosity.

Distance Requirements: Marks shall be placed on the landing mat at the following distances: ½, 1, 1½, and 2 meters from the horse. Corresponding deductions/virtuosity shall be as follows:

If the gymnast lands between:	
0 and ½ meter from the horse	0.5 deduction
½ and 1 meter	0.3 deduction
1 and 1½ meters	0 deduction

Landing: The minimum landing deduction is **0.2**. This means that any landing that is not "stuck" would receive **at least** a 0.2 deduction

Parallel Bars

Designated Virtuous Elements (each worth 0.1, up to 0.6 total)

1. Swing backward in part 2. to 45 degrees above horizontal
2. Back uprise in part 4. to 45 degrees above horizontal
3. Swing backward in part 5. to handstand held 2 seconds
4. Straight arm, straddled press to handstand in part 7.
5. Front uprise in part 8. with hips at shoulder height
6. Swing backward in part 9. to nominal handstand
7. Stutz dismount in part 10. to 45 degrees above horizontal at the turn

Horizontal Bar

Designated Virtuous Elements (each worth **0.1, up to 0.6** total)

1. Cast forward in part 1. to 45 degrees above horizontal
2. Free hip circle in part 2. to nominal handstand
3. Swing forward with half turn in part 3. to 45 degrees above horizontal
4. Swing forward in part 4. to 45 degrees above horizontal
5. Swing backward in part 5. to 45 degrees above horizontal
6. Cast in part 6. to nominal handstand
7. Giant underswing in part 8. through handstand
8. Underbar shoot in part 9. to 45 degrees above horizontal
9. Swing backward in part 9. to 45 degrees above horizontal
10. Tucked flyaway in part 10. with hips well above bar height

LEVEL IV

Floor Exercise

Designated Virtuous Elements (each worth **0.1**)

1. Kick to handstand in part 2. held 2 seconds
2. Straight arm back extension roll in part 3.
3. Straddle press to handstand in part 4.
4. Straddle push to handstand in part 4. held 2 seconds
5. Pancake in part 7. with 160 degree or more straddle with chest on floor
6. Straight arm back extension roll in part 8.
7. Side scale in part 9. with at least a 135 degree straddle of the legs
8. Exceptional height on the stretched rebound in part 10.

Major elements summary

Front handspring to stand
Kick to handstand
Back extension roll, lower to straddle stand
Straight arm, straddled push to handstand
Cartwheel, half turn, cartwheel
Prone fall, turn over, lower to pancake
Piked forward bend to back extension roll
Handstand, step down to side lunge, side scale
Round off, flip flop, punch

Pommel Horse

Designated Virtuous Elements (0.1 each time **up to 0.6**)

1. Body extended throughout loops and/or circular movements (body angle of 135 degrees or more)
2. Ninety degree or greater straddle maintained in single leg work

Major elements summary

Loop
Single leg travel up
Stride support swing
Single leg travel down
One-half downhill circle

Rings

Designated Virtuous Elements (each worth **0.1, up to 0.6** total)

1. Pull up in part 1. with straight body
2. Pull out of hang in part 3. with straight body
3. Inlocate in part 5. with straight body and continuous movement
4. Inlocate in part 6. with straight body and continuous movement
5. Backward swing in part 7. well above horizontal with heel-leading action
6. Dislocate in part 8. with shoulders ring height
7. Swing forward in part 9. to well above horizontal
8. Swing backward in part 9. to well above horizontal
9. Tucked flyaway in part 10. with hips above ring height at release

Vault

Required Spotter: There is a required spotter between the board and the horse. If there is no spotter, a **0.5** deduction will result.

Height Requirement: The hips of the gymnast must rise 1 meter at the peak of flight and after contact with the horse to receive no height deduction. Showing extreme height could be awarded **up to 0.2** virtuousity.

Distance Requirements: Marks shall be placed on the landing mat at the following distances: ½, 1, 1½, and 2 meters from the horse. Corresponding deductions/virtuosity shall be as follows:

If the gymnast lands between:	
0 and ½ meter from the horse	0.5 deduction
½ and 1 meter	0.3 deduction
1 and 1½ meters	0 deduction
1½ and 2 meters	+0.1 bonus
over 2 meters	+0.2 bonus

Landing: The minimum landing deduction is **0.2**. This means that any landing that is not "stuck" would receive **at least** a 0.2 deduction.

Horse Height: All gymnasts have the option of vaulting at the lowest horse height setting.

Parallel Bars

Designated Virtuous Elements (each worth **0.1, up to 0.6** total)

1. Back uprise in part 2. to 45 degrees above horizontal
2. Swing backward in part 4. to nominal handstand
3. Straight arm press to handstand (no hold) in part 6.
4. Back uprise in part 7. to 45 degrees above horizontal
5. Swing backward in part 9. to nominal handstand
6. Stutz dismount in part 10. to 30 degrees above horizontal at the turn

Horizontal Bar

Designated Virtuous Elements (each worth **0.1, up to 0.6**)

1. Cast forward in part 1. to horizontal
2. Swing backward in part 2. to horizontal
3. Swing forward with half turn in part 3. to horizontal
4. Swing forward in part 4. to horizontal
5. Swing backward in part 5. to horizontal
6. Kip to immediate cast in part 7.
7. Cast in part 8. to 45 degrees above horizontal
8. Free hip circle in part 9.
9. Underbar shoot with half turn dismount with hips well above bar height and with body stretched and free of the bar

LEVEL V

Floor Exercise

Virtuosity (0.2 maximum)

1. Straight arms in rolls (2. and 5.)	0.1 each
2. Extreme flexibility in straddle sit (5.)	0.1
3. Exceptional control and flexibility in scale (3.)	0.1
4. Extreme amplitude and control in straight jump (9.)	0.1
5. Press to handstand, lower to headstand (7.)	0.1
6. As per F.I.G. Code	up to 0.2 each time

Major Elements In Simple Terms

Hurdle
Cartwheel, cartwheel
Kick handstand, roll out
Side scale
Prone fall
Back straddle roll
Pancake
Roll back and forward to straddle stand
Press to headstand
Roll forward to straight jump
Round off, straight jump

Pommel Horse

Virtuosity (0.2 maximum)

1. Maintaining continuous rhythm throughout	0.1
2. Maintaining straddle greater than 90 degrees throughout skill when required	0.1 each time
3. Leg cuts and/or swings well above the required amplitude	0.1 each time
4. As per F.I.G. Code	up to 0.2 each time

Major Elements In Simple Terms

Jump to stride support
Single leg uphill side travel
2 straddle support swings
Single leg downhill side travel
Single leg cut dismount

Rings

General Comments

1. All positions that call for a momentary hold must clearly show the position before moving on. However, positions must not be held more than 1 second.
2. *The amplitude that is required for underswings is when the body is at a 45 degree angle below horizontal, with some shoulder elevation on the forward swing.

Virtuosity (0.2 maximum)

1. Swings in 2, 4, and 5 done above horizontal	0.1 each time
2. Flyaway with hips well above ring height (6.)	0.1
3. As per F.I.G. Code	up to 0.2 each time

Vault

General Comments

Both height and distance requirements are based upon the size of the individual gymnast.

Height requirement: The hips should rise one half the height of the gymnast.

Distance requirement: Point of landing should be 1½ times the height of the gymnast from the horse.

Virtuosity (0.2 maximum)

1. Showing extreme height and distance in the post-flight	up to 0.2

Parallel Bars

Virtuosity (0.2 maximum)

1. Feet together at horizontal before straddle support (1., 4.)	0.1 each
2. Forward support swings (3., 5.) above horizontal	0.1 each
3. Backward support swings (3., 4., 5.) above 45 degrees	0.1 each
4. Dismount above 45 degrees (6.)	0.1
5. As per F.I.G. Code	up to 0.2 each time

Horizontal Bar

Virtuosity (0.2 maximum)

1. Pull over with straight legs (2.)	0.1
2. Cast above horizontal (3.)	0.1
3. Single leg knee swing with forward leg straight throughout and without touching bar (5.)	0.1
4. Cast above horizontal on dismount (7.)	0.1
5. As per F.I.G. Code	up to 0.2 each time

Learn the rules for all your favorite sports with Perigee's popular *Sports Rules in Pictures* series!

Illustrated throughout with clearly captioned, easy-to-follow drawings of actual playing situations, these handy guides to the rules of America's favorite sports are ideal for players, weekend athletes, and fans alike. For the last word on any dispute, these guides will provide the answer.

Baseball Rules in Pictures
By G. Jacobs and J. R. McCrory
This ready guide is a quick and easy way to learn baseball rules and check decisions. Nearly 200 captioned drawings cover sections on pitching, batting, baserunning, and fielding. Included is a foreword by legendary umpire Ron Luciano and the complete Official Rules of Baseball.

Official Little League Baseball ® Rules in Pictures
Introduction by Dr. Creighton J. Hale,
President, Little League Baseball
Incorporating more than 150 illustrations, the full text of Little League's Official Playing Rules, and all the latest rule changes, this straightforward guide is an indispensable handbook for the two million youngsters who play Little League baseball every year. Parents, coaches, managers, and umpires will find the book an essential companion on the field or in the stands.

Softball Rules in Pictures
By G. Jacobs McCrory
Revised by Michael J. Brown
Over 90 all-new drawings and a new, easy-to-follow text clarify the latest rules from the Amateur Softball Association of America in chapters on equipment, pitching, batting, and baserunning. The complete text of the rules is included along with umpire signals to help players and spectators follow the game more easily.

Football Rules in Pictures
Edited by Don Schiffer and Lud Duroska
Both stadium and armchair football fans will welcome this newly revised handbook including the latest Official National Football League Digest of Rules with its Summary of Penalties, pro, college, and high school interpretations of the game rules, and quick-reference guide to officials' signals.

Basketball Rules in Pictures
Edited by A. G. Jacobs
Profuse illustrations, captions, and text provide a complete explanation of the essential regulations of basketball, followed by a section on basic basketball play and patterns and a helpful guide to officials' signals.

Hockey Rules in Pictures
By The National Hockey League
Incorporating the complete text of the NHL Official Rules Book and the latest rule changes in use today, this handy book clearly and carefully explains goals and scoring, face-offs, high-sticking, board-checking, falling on the puck, and more. Includes a quick-reference guide to officials' signals.

Amateur Wrestling Rules in Pictures
By Michael Brown
With its hundreds of different techniques, wrestling is one of the most demanding and complicated sports to understand. With helpful stop-action illustrations and easy-to-read language, this practical guide explains wrestling's international rules, weight classes, officials' signals, boundary regulations, scoring, and much more.

Volleyball Rules in Pictures
By Michael Brown
Here is the first fully illustrated guide to America's fastest-growing sport, featuring the complete text of the Official United States Volleyball Rules as approved by the U.S. Volleyball Association, a handy guide to officials' hand signals, and over 150 line drawings and captions that explain every aspect of the game.

Golf Rules in Pictures
An Official Publication of the United States Golf Association
Introduction by Arnold Palmer
Scores of clearly captioned pictures cover golf rules from hazards, penalty strokes, and scoring to the number of clubs allowed and what to do when you accidentally hit an opponent's ball. Included is the complete text of The Rules of Golf as approved by the U.S. Golf Association and the Royal and Ancient Golf Club of St. Andrews, Scotland.

Tennis Rules and Techniques in Pictures
By Michael J. Brown
This authoritative guide explains and illustrates the rules of tennis—including doubles play—and describes the basic techniques of tennis, providing instructions on the various grips and service and advice on court tactics. The complete text of the official rules of the United States Tennis Association is included.

Track and Field Rules in Pictures
By Michael Brown
This guide covers the often confusing rules for competition, and everything the athlete needs to know about procedures for relay racing, foot faults, disqualification, proper approaches for jumping events, lane changing, scratch lines, false starts, and much more.

Soccer Rules in Pictures
By Michael Brown
Complete with the official NCAA Men's Soccer Rules, this is the indispensable guide to learning about the game of soccer. Find out what the penalties are for the various rules infractions, and learn the special rules that apply to goalkeepers, and what the referee's signals mean. Check the rules, read about the intricacies of the game, and become an expert on soccer whether you're a player or a fan.

Ordering *Sports Rules in Pictures* is easy and convenient. Just call 1-800-631-8571 or send your order to:
The Putnam Publishing Group
390 Murray Hill Parkway, Dept. B
East Rutherford, NJ 07073
Also available at your local bookstore or wherever paperbacks are sold.

			PRICE	
			U.S.	CANADA
_____	Baseball Rules in Pictures	399-51597	$7.95	$10.50
_____	Official Little League Baseball® Rules in Pictures	399-51531	7.95	10.50
_____	Softball Rules in Pictures	399-51356	6.95	9.25
_____	Football Rules in Pictures	399-51479	7.95	10.50
_____	Basketball Rules in Pictures	399-51590	7.95	10.50
_____	Hockey Rules in Pictures	399-51480	7.95	10.50
_____	Amateur Wrestling Rules in Pictures	399-51589	7.95	10.50
_____	Volleyball Rules in Pictures	399-51537	7.95	10.50
_____	Golf Rules in Pictures	399-51438	7.95	10.50
_____	Tennis Rules and Techniques in Pictures	399-51405	7.95	10.50
_____	Track and Field Rules in Pictures	399-51620	7.95	10.50
_____	Soccer Rules in Pictures	399-51647	7.95	10.50

Subtotal $_____
*Postage & Handling $_____
Sales Tax $_____
(CA, NJ, NY, PA)
Total Amount Due $_____
Payable in U.S. Funds
(No cash orders accepted)

*Postage & Handling: $1.00 for 1 book, 25¢ for each additional book up to a maximum of $3.50.

Please send me the titles I've checked above. Enclosed is my:

☐ check ☐ money order

Please charge my

☐ Visa ☐ MasterCard

Card # _____ Expiration date _____

Signature as on charge card _____

Name _____

Address _____

City _____ State _____ Zip _____

Please allow six weeks for delivery. Prices subject to change without notice.